Advance praise for *future* WEALTH

"The Internet revolution has so altered the economic foundations of post-industrial society that entirely new ways of looking at wealth are evolving. *Future Wealth* discusses the impact of global electronic markets on the individual investor as well as on the corporation and provides a valuable guide to the far-ranging, sometimes daunting financial and social transformations ahead."

— DR. HENRY A. KISSINGER, FORMER SECRETARY OF STATE

"*Future Wealth* is a masterpiece, full of breakthrough insights and bold recommendations. A must read for both individuals and companies that intend to succeed in the new economy."

— WALTER V. SHIPLEY, CHAIRMAN OF THE BOARD, CHASE MANHATTAN CORPORATION

"Whether you are self-employed, an Internet entrepreneur, a manager in a large corporation, or a policy wonk, this book is essential reading if you want to master the new economy."

— KEN LAY, CHAIRMAN OF THE BOARD AND CEO, ENRON CORPORATION

"In the digital age, what you earn is far less important than what you are worth. This eye-opening, provocative book illustrates the real value of dot.self and shows how to buy and sell derivatives of mental capital. Read it and gain an appetite for risk."

— NICHOLAS NEGROPONTE, COFOUNDER AND DIRECTOR, MIT MEDIA LAB

"As individuals become more aware of their wealth, and more responsible for managing it, our society will change. *Future Wealth* offers a compelling vision of our financial future."

—ART RYAN, CHAIRMAN OF THE BOARD AND CEO, PRUDENTIAL INSURANCE COMPANY OF AMERICA

"Davis and Meyer, in a sound analysis, have mapped out many astounding and profound societal changes likely to result from the Internet revolution."

—FREDERICK W. SMITH, CHAIRMAN OF THE BOARD AND CEO, FEDERAL EXPRESS

"*Future Wealth* offers a mind-stretching look at how an efficient, transparent, Internet-connected economy could work. It helps you see how the unthinkable might actually be possible."

—CLAYTON M. CHRISTENSEN, ASSOCIATE PROFESSOR, HARVARD BUSINESS SCHOOL, AND AUTHOR OF *The Innovator's Dilemma*

"*Future Wealth* is a major, necessary book for both business strategists and public policy makers. Davis and Meyer offer a compelling vision of economic growth for all people, companies, and societies."

—VERNON E. JORDAN, JR., SENIOR MANAGING DIRECTOR, LAZARD FRERES & CO.

"A terrific read. Challenges even the most sophisticated assumptions about wealth, risk, and value in a connected economy."

—JIM C. CURVEY, PRESIDENT AND COO, FIDELITY

"A provocative book that stimulates readers to think about how the revolution in information technology opens up new contracting possibilities for their human and financial capital."

—BOB KAPLAN, PROFESSOR, HARVARD BUSINESS SCHOOL, AND COAUTHOR OF *The Balanced Scorecard*

"Davis and Meyer have done it again. In their last bestseller, *Blur*, they described the connected economy from 25,000 feet. Now, in *Future Wealth*, they bore down to ground zero, exploring the implications of the new economy for personal investors, private citizens, individual firms, and even governments. The boldness of the thinking and the clarity of the writing put *Future Wealth* in a class by itself."

—THOMAS PETZINGER JR., COLUMNIST,
The Wall Street Journal

"*Future Wealth* is a wide-ranging and provocative book that will make you think. It may well reorder your personal business strategies as you negotiate the rapids of today's global economy."

—ALEX TROTMAN, RETIRED CHAIRMAN OF THE BOARD
AND CEO, FORD MOTOR COMPANY

"Two decades of formidable restructuring, innovation, and wealth creation have left everyone puzzled about how to fit into the new scheme of things, how to avoid being left out, and how to avoid being suckered. This book is a formidable manual on how to make sense of risk and opportunities. Unlike the get-rich-quick literature, it will make you work smarter as well as harder. A must for anyone who wants to go beyond the clichés and quacks."

—RUDI DORNBUSCH, FORD PROFESSOR OF ECONOMICS AND
INTERNATIONAL MANAGEMENT, MIT

"Financial institutions secured by intellectual capital? Mutual funds representing shares in people? *Future Wealth* offers an intelligent and provocative look at the implications of an emerging 'connected' economy, where risk becomes opportunity and human capital is more bankable than tangible assets. This book will change how you think about your job, your company, and doing business in the new century."

—STEVEN M. H. WALLMAN, FORMER SEC COMMISSIONER,
AND CHAIRMAN OF THE BOARD AND CEO, FOLIO[*fn*] INC.

"Davis and Meyer show us that the Internet doesn't just change business—it will transform wealth, employment, and social institutions as well. *Future Wealth* is a compelling book, important for both private citizens and policy makers."

—THE RIGHT HONORABLE BRIAN MULRONEY,
FORMER PRIME MINISTER OF CANADA

"Davis and Meyer chart the transfer of value from hard assets in property, plant, and equipment to the new drivers of wealth such as intellectual property and creative, innovative people. *Future Wealth* is superb."

—PETER MUNK, CHAIRMAN OF THE BOARD,
BARRICK GOLD CORPORATION

future WEALTH

OTHER BOOKS BY STAN DAVIS AND CHRISTOPHER MEYER

Blur (1998)

OTHER BOOKS BY STAN DAVIS

Future Perfect (1996, 1987)
The Monster Under the Bed, with Jim Botkin (1994)
2020 Vision, with Bill Davidson (1991)
Managing Corporate Culture (1984)
Managing and Organizing Multinational Corporations (1979)
Matrix, with Paul Lawrence (1977)
Workers and Managers in Latin America, with Louis Goodman (1972)
Comparative Management (1971)

STAN DAVIS
CHRISTOPHER MEYER

future
WEALTH

HARVARD BUSINESS SCHOOL PRESS
BOSTON, MASSACHUSETTS

Library of Congress Cataloging-in-Publication Data

Davis, Stanley M.
    Future wealth / Stan Davis, Christopher Meyer.
      p. cm.
    Includes bibliographical references and index.
    ISBN 1-57851-194-1 (alk. paper)
    1. Wealth. 2. Income. 3. Equality. I. Meyer, Christopher, 1948– II. Title.
  HC79.W4 D377 2000
  330.1'6--dc21

                                          99-059014

"A few men own capital; and that few avoid labor themselves, and with their capital, hire, or buy, another few to labor for them. A large majority belong to neither class—neither work for others, nor have others working for them. . . . And their case is almost if not quite the general rule. The prudent, penniless beginner in the world labors for wages for awhile, saves a surplus with which to buy tools or land, for himself; then labors on his own account for another while, and at length hires another beginner to help him. This, say its advocates, is free labor—the just and generous, and prosperous system, which opens the way for all—gives hope to all, and energy, and progress, and improvement of condition to all."

—ABRAHAM LINCOLN, 1859

Contents

An Invitation to the Reader   xi

PART I   FOUNDATIONS

1   From Income to Wealth
    How the Tail Wags the Dog   3

2   From Early to Late Information Age
    Three Forces of Change   15

3   From Barter to Bloomberg
    Trading Risk and Human Capital   25

PART II   INDIVIDUALS

4   From Paycheck to Portfolio
    Know Thy Worth   39

5   From Corporate Cog to Market Cap
    Maximizing the Value of Your Human Capital   45

6   From Worker to Player
    Securitizing Your Human Capital   57

7   From Risk as Problem to Risk as Opportunity
    Profiting from Uncertainty   67

PART III   COMPANIES

8   From SBUs to SRUs
    Managing Strategic Risk   81

9   From Inside to Outside
    Running Your Organization by Marketplace Rules   93

10 From Payrolls to Portfolios
    Transforming Human Resource Management   101

11 From Vesting to Investing
    *Maximizing the Market Value of
    Your Human Capital*   109

12 From Past to Future
    Measures That Matter   119

PART IV   SOCIETY

13 From Marx to Markets
    Creating Middle-Class Wealth   127

14 From Debtors' Prison to Chapter 11
    Higher Wires, Stronger Nets   137

15 From Safety to Risk
    Cultural Values for a Connected World   149

PART V   HORIZONS

16 Twenty Perfect Futures   161

    Notes   171

    Acknowledgments   183

    Index   185

    About the Authors   201

An Invitation to the Reader

Our conversations began in 1988, as Stan was writing 2020 *Vision*. They deepened after Chris became the Director of the Ernst & Young Center for Business Innovation and Stan joined for a day a week over the last four years as Senior Research Fellow there. The two of us began the collaboration that eventually would produce our previous book, *Blur,* and now *Future Wealth*.

We established a Web site for *Blur* to continue the dialogue about value creation in the real economy, where we produce and consume goods and services. Now we ask you to enrich the content further and move our conversation into the financial economy, where we earn incomes, finance businesses, and trade securities. Please note our Web site: <**www.future-wealth.com**>. And share your thoughts there as you read these words and ponder your own future wealth.

Our goal is not to have the last word on *Future Wealth,* or on any other subject. In the spirit of the connected economy, we strive to connect—ourselves with you, you with each other, and all of us with the economic issues that define our times and our futures. Connect with us, and lob a grenade or two. Our conversation with each other is always respectful but not always polite.

We hope to encourage communication among our readers, our clients, and ourselves. We also hope that, as we expand the conversation, you will fill in the missing pieces of our understanding and provide us with more and better examples and counterexamples, just as we help you understand where this new economic infrastructure is taking us. Your decision to join the debate will enrich us all. Sharing, not scarcity, creates value.

So, we hope that you'll log on as you read on. Teach us as we tell you what we know: That's the paradigm of learning in an interconnected world. You'll find that *Future Wealth* has five parts. In the first, we outline our three themes and the economic forces that are driving them. Then, in parts II through IV, we look at how the themes play out for individuals, businesses, and society. We close with twenty "Perfect Futures" on the horizon (part V).

PART I

foundations

WE ARE BUILDING the connected economy, in which businesses succeed by pursuing speed, connectivity, and intangible value. The rules of business have changed, and have already profoundly affected the markets for goods and services.

Now, the changed rules are affecting wealth. Communications are so pervasive that anyone anywhere can trade anything, from coffee futures to attic junk. The most important form of capital is human capital; people are beginning to see themselves as assets. The social rules governing wealth that worked in the stable physical world are creaking.

As these trends unfold, we will see three enormous changes affect our economy and society. First, we will come to see risk not as a threat (as in the physical world) but as an opportunity (as in the financial world). Second, we will find efficient markets developing for everything, including our scarcest resource: human capital. Third, we will need to develop new social safety nets so that society willingly takes all the risk that it can afford—and earns the highest possible returns.

FROM INCOME TO WEALTH
How the Tail Wags the Dog

Molecular biologists are up 3 points, and economists down ¼, in moderate trading.

My teenage daughter, a millionaire on paper, is considering going public (but I can't retire yet).

The Wall Street Journal *reports that 45 percent of the American workforce are free agents.*

Fortune *observes that market indices rather than human resource policies directly determine the compensation of more than half the workforce.*

The Supreme Court rules that consumers' "clickstreams" (the paths people take as they surf from Web site to Web site) are their private property and that misuse of this information is a federal offense.

The last pupil in America is wired—wirelessed, actually—for broadband Net access.

After years of debate, Congress finally passes laws allowing people to decide how much risk to take in their social insurance accounts.

LABOR MARKETS. Wealth. Employment. Management. Property rights. Education. Risk. The old ways no longer hold. New ones tumble in. It is a liminal moment.

The new mantra is "The Internet changes everything," and it's even truer than we can imagine. The foundation of our economy has shifted, and with the new foundation has come a new set of rules about wealth. Anything is possible. Even trading molecular biologists.

In fact, the future caught up with us while writing this page. We had written, *"The American Medical Association adds day trading to its list of recognized addictions."* But then, in August 1999, the American Psychological Association (APA) reported that more than 11 million Web users, or 6 percent, "suffer from some form of addiction to the World Wide Web."[1]

You might be asking, "What are Stan and Chris talking about? Investing and trading in humans just as we do in corporate securities? A financial market for human capital? Are they kidding?"

No, we're not. Our economic foundation is changing dramatically, and so are all the rules we have about wealth. How we make it and build it, control it, and spread it about are all changing.

We read every day about individuals who start dot.com businesses from their college dorm, do an IPO six months later, and become fabulously wealthy. Human capital—your daughter's smarts, a scientist's inventiveness, your knowledge and experience—is the currency of future wealth.

At the same time, corporate America is writing new rules. After a decade of reworking the old ways (reducing, reengineering, rewiring), and now the rush into the new business models for the Internet world, we can next expect significantly new forms of management and organization.

What remains undiscovered, beneath the headlines of me.coms and software billionaires, are the deeper structural shifts in financial markets and in economic value. These shifts are profoundly altering the nature of wealth. By wealth we mean not just the investment portfolios of rich people, but the stock of value that individuals, companies, and societies generate in a successful economy. Wealth means investments in securities, but also taxation, education, industrial plants, and social institutions. To understand how wealth will change in the future, we'll start with the past.

THE CONNECTED ECONOMY

In agrarian times, wealth meant land. In industrial times, it meant factories. Recently, information replaced industrial capacity as the primary means of creating wealth, and now the economic foundation is shifting yet again. Today's e-commerce strategies and Net-based businesses are evidence of this happening—they are the current development of the connected economy.

The changes are grounded in the fundamentals of the universe—time, space, and mass. We experience them in everyday life as speed, connectivity, and intangibles. Speed shows itself in drastically shortened product lifetimes, customer response cycles, management decision making, and the end of equilibrium as a management mind-set. Connectivity, hooking up everybody and everything electronically, has made distance—space—irrelevant, and put any useful information where it is needed, instantly. Intangibles—such as software, information, services, and most recently, human capital—have replaced hard goods—mass—as the most valuable and fastest-growing part of the economy.

The shift to intangibles happened in three waves. In the first wave, from the 1950s into the 1970s, service businesses grew faster than product-based ones. Services were 31 percent of the U.S. national output in 1950, increased to 42 percent by 1970 and 46 percent by 1980, and reached 55 percent by 1998.[2]

In the second wave, from the 1970s through the 1990s, the core of today's $1.5 trillion worldwide computer and communications industries has shifted from hardware to software and information services.[3] Seen as barely more than an accessory in the 1970s, software now dominates the computer industry, and products and services alike are made of and by software.

The third and current wave of intangible value, the rise of human and intellectual capital as the most highly valued resource of the late information age, began in the 1990s and will continue for the next few decades.

These three principles define the connected economy:

Speed: Constant change is healthier than stability.

Connectivity: Open systems thrive, closed ones wither.

Intangibles: The virtual trumps the physical.

THE NATURE OF WEALTH

In our previous book, *Blur*, we wrote that the production and consumption of goods and services—what economists call the "real" dimension of the economy—was changing to reflect these principles. In *Future Wealth*, we turn to the financial side of the economy. Don't confuse this with the financial services industry, with its banks, brokerages, and insurance companies, although this sector will be profoundly affected. We focus here on the financial aspects of all people, business, and society. We're accustomed to the financial aspects of business.

Today, however, as connectivity proliferates, anyone can trade any-thing of value electronically. Soon every individual will participate in finance—defined as trading risk—as both trad*er* and trad*ee*.

The definition of wealth remains, as always, the means by which we fulfill our desires. As the saying goes, you are wealthy if you want no more than what you have, whether you grasp for fame, for-tune, friends, or followers. In economic terms, this translates into material possessions and the means to attain them. In social and political terms, it translates into greater freedoms, and the means to attain them. To fare well, we need a new mind-set for the way we work and earn; spend and save; plan our mortgages, taxes, and investments; and take responsibility for our own development.

This holds equally for individuals, companies, and societies.

Wealth has a life cycle: It is created and accumulated; then it is distributed, whether through taxation, dividends, or inheritance. At any moment, we can take a snapshot of where wealth is being con-trolled. Each of these aspects of wealth is mutating.

Wealth Creation and Accumulation

While the real economy creates wealth by producing goods and services, the financial dimension does so by bearing, trading, and managing risks. This difference is enormous.

For individuals, it's the difference between our labor (real) and our investments (financial). People accumulate real wealth through both their tangible possessions, such as cars, houses, and furnish-ings, and their intangible ones, such as their knowledge and rela-tionships. But they build financial wealth—their net worth—by bearing risks in their 401(k)s and investment portfolios.

Every asset has a value, and every value is at risk. Many of us sell one home and buy another, recognizing that every piece of real estate has both upside and downside financial risk. Few actively set about trading houses as a way to make profits. More of us, however, are borrowing against our homes in order to trade financial assets based on our judgment of whether they'll rise or fall in value. In other words, we trade risk.

For companies, we're discussing the difference between the products and services they offer (real) and the cash flows they generate (financial). Real wealth lies in tangibles, such as factories, and in intangibles, such as customer relationships. But if you want to see a company's financial worth, then look at its share price. That's what companies themselves do, and that's why they put so much effort into financial engineering, massaging earnings, and so forth, to keep analysts enthusiastic and investors bullish.

And for societies, it's the difference between the GDP's growing annually by 3 percent (real) and the Dow Jones Industrial Average's growing—or shrinking—by 20 percent. It's also the difference between the quality of a society's infrastructure—its roads, hospitals, and the like—and its borrowing capacities and currency reserves.

In all three domains, making money is starting to be as important as making stuff. Money takes on a life of its own. As we've seen in recent history, currency crises can drive the real economy into sharp recessions, as in Mexico, Thailand, Malaysia, and Indonesia. Businesses can be similarly constrained by their liquidity. And individuals save or consume, depending on their own investment performance as well as their appetites for risk.

Traditionally, most economists have considered the real sector primary and the financial sector secondary. In August 1999, this perspective reversed, as Federal Reserve Chairman Alan Greenspan explained to Congress. Here's how the *New York Times* reported Greenspan's testimony:

> *"We no longer have the luxury to look primarily to the flow of goods and services"* when making decisions about interest rates, Mr. Greenspan said. In effect, he was labeling what he called the *"extraordinary increase in stock prices over the past five years"* as one

of the major economic forces capable of pushing up the inflation rate. Traditionally, a run-up in stock prices has been viewed as reflecting a strong economy and profitable companies. The economy drove the market. Now the opposite is more and more the case, Mr. Greenspan suggested.[4]

In other words, as we create the connected economy, the economic action—the accumulation of wealth—is shifting from the real economy to the financial, for two main reasons.

In the short term, investors perceive the connected economy as an extraordinary opportunity to create real future value and are buying into it, bidding up the stock market and creating current financial wealth. There is undoubtedly some inflation of asset values, but the financial markets are correctly recognizing growth opportunities. The *rate of growth* in value may be temporary, but not the billions of dollars of market capitalization which will ultimately be sustained by the continuing creation of value in the real sector.

Longer term, the information economy's form of capital—information, knowledge, and talent—can be leveraged indefinitely at much lower costs than can the financial capital needed to build steel mills in the industrial age. The amount of financial capital required is much smaller, which is lowering the amount of capital needed and thus its cost. And, unlike a factory, information's capacity is almost unlimited. The wealth from movies or computer games comes from almost pure margin as more and more people use them, a phenomenon often called "increasing returns."

The connected economy is built on increasing-returns businesses, software most of all, and therefore takes less physical capital to produce a given quantity of economic value. This is one way the economy becomes intangible. Microsoft's sales-to-physical-assets ratio is 12.26, whereas U.S. Steel's is now only 1.96.[5] This means that financial capital is becoming less scarce, the cost of capital is falling, and the price of entry to new businesses is lower. These factors will continue to hold true whatever the fate of the Internet stock run-up, so don't dismiss them even if, by the time you read this, price-earnings ratios are depressed. To be an entrepreneur, you won't have to create a low-risk business plan to get a lot of money. You can create a high-risk one and fund it yourself, or with a friend. The ease of raising the required cash or of self-funding new ventures in turn will change the distribution of wealth in society.

Wealth Distribution

Any discussion of wealth invariably leads to the gap between haves and have-nots, and future wealth certainly doesn't promise the end of inequality. But it does mean that over time wealth will no longer be just for the wealthy. A major shift in distribution is already beginning within our own minds, and our pockets will follow. Instead of standing on the sidelines watching the elite get richer, a broad segment of society will be on the playing field.

Almost all of us know how much we make (income), but it's only a slight exaggeration to say that almost none of us know our net worth. Those who have inherited wealth and the financially enlightened few understand the important difference between income and net worth. They focus on the latter and make it work for them. What they earn directly is not their primary financial concern.

Not too long ago, a lawyer brought this home to us by saying, "No matter how much or little you make, it's still only walking-around money." The statement is both arrogant and accurate. His remark underscores the increased importance of "unearned" income and its growing contribution to people's accumulation of net worth. Earned income consists of the salaries, wages, and tips you work for. Unearned income is the additional wealth created by putting your assets to work for you. The more that wealth accumulates in the form of financial assets, and the more those shares and other securities appreciate in value, the more wealth is created, not as earned, but as *un*earned income.

Unearned income from interest, dividends, capital gains, pensions, and annuities has become steadily more important to U.S. households For every dollar made in earned income in 1975—that is, taxable income earned from wages, businesses, and unemployment insurance—U.S. households got 13 cents in unearned income. By 1997, this figure almost doubled, to 25 cents.[6] As wealth becomes more liquid and takes the form of financial rather than real assets, the middle-class appetite for risk is growing. The more unearned income that people make, the more risk they are bearing.

In 1990, investors placed $44 billion in new money into mutual funds. In 1998, the figure reached $477 billion.[7] According to the *Wall Street Journal*, 80 million Americans, or 52 percent of households, own investments.[8] Paychecks will always matter, bull markets come to an end, financial bubbles burst, and periods of poor stock market performance interrupt the growth of unearned income. But the data suggest an irreversible trend: The source of financial wealth is shifting from money that you work for toward money that works for you. Unearned income is growing, and more people have it. Wealth is becoming middle class.

By "middle class" we mean individuals and households not rich enough to live without working, but with enough income to save regularly. Years ago we might have called them "well-to-do." Today, the sustained boom in the United States has moved some poorer families into this category, though the distance between the richest and the poorest continues to grow. In our discussion, what matters most is not the gap, but the proportion of the society we can call middle class and above.

As society as a whole gets richer, people will benefit more from the wealth they previously accumulated and will depend less on their current wealth creation. This feeds on itself: When wealth grows faster than income, unearned income is an ever-larger proportion of total income. To ride this trend, you must appreciate net worth as the *source* of wealth, not merely the outcome.

Wealth has been accumulating for a long time, but even in the advanced economies not everyone is emancipated yet. We are all living off capital generated in the past, and most of it is not on the books. Pasteur, for example, accumulated intellectual capital that still reduces misery and lengthens life, but it is not captured in any financial accounting, as if it were fully depreciated and obsolete. As markets get more connected, this accumulation has been building in financial terms, and control of it is becoming more widely distributed.

Wealth Control

The control of wealth is tilting from institutions to individuals.

In early industrial times, control of wealth moved from the few landowners to the robber barons who controlled the new scarce resource: credit. In the late industrial era, managers controlled corporate wealth without owning it. Then, the rapid growth of retirement plans and the crunching power of computers made employee pension funds major controllers of the economy's wealth.

Still, neither the employees—those who owned the plans and for whose benefit the pension funds operated—nor the unions—those who helped workers gain their retirement benefits—gained control of the wealth. Instead, control went to the financial analysts who advised the plans and the fund managers who ran them.

With four distinct economic periods (late agrarian, early and late industrial, and early information), we have had four different groups in control of the nation's wealth: *from landed gentry, to owners, to managers, to pension funds*. Now, with the democratization of financial information, individuals are taking more responsibility for managing their own wealth. The power is shifting yet again, this time to you and me. Brace yourself.

Many individuals already have the same on-line access to their retirement assets, whether through their benefits department or e-Schwab, as they do to their Amazon orders and FedEx shipments.

We can safely expect the control of wealth to shift yet again, this time to *individuals*, who will increasingly own and manage their own funds, bear and track their own risk, in order to accumulate net future wealth.

People have become the custodians of their economic futures through vehicles such as 401(k)s, Keogh plans, and IRAs. Individuals, not their employers, are taking responsibility for their futures, and managing their pensions is one example.

NET NET

The changes we're talking about are nothing short of momentous. Consider them again:

Wealth creation becomes more financial than real.

Wealth accumulation shifts from earned to unearned.

Middle-class wealth is no longer an oxymoron.

Control of wealth shifts from institutions to individuals.

The shift to the connected economy is already revolutionizing the infrastructure of the real economy. And so the ways in which wealth is created, accumulated, distributed, and controlled must change, too. Wealth affects not just the wealthy, but every one of us and every aspect of our society—how we're paid and taxed, what risks our businesses take, how our society invests in itself. Examples are shown in the table "Real and Financial Wealth." Future wealth isn't just about personal investing. It's about a major transformation in the economic life of individuals, the rules of business, and the welfare of society.

Real and Financial Wealth

Wealth has two natures: one real, the other financial. For individuals, this duality means the money earned on the job and on Wall Street. Company wealth and society wealth have similar origins. As the table shows, all three constituencies accumulate, distribute, and control wealth of both kinds. Parts II, III, and IV deal with each group in turn.

PART I FOUNDATIONS	*Wealth Creation*	*Wealth Accumulation*	*Wealth Distribution*	*Wealth Control*
PART II INDIVIDUALS	Work and productivity	Household possessions Knowledge Social networks	Last will and testament	Own/rent home
	Investment income	Net worth (401(k), market portfolio)	Philanthropy	Vested pensions
PART III COMPANIES	Production of goods and services	Factories Customer relationships	Pricing	M&A Capital expenditures and budgets
	Profits	Sharehold equity	Stock options Dividend payments	Stock ownership
PART IV SOCIETY	GDP/GNP Education	Rule of law Public trust Democratic institutions Roads	"Pork barrel" politics Medicaid	Property rights
	Stock markets	Currency reserves and public debt	Taxation Welfare	Regulatory controls Bankruptcy laws

FROM EARLY TO LATE INFORMATION AGE
Three Forces of Change

For a dollar a month, an Ohio insurance company will rent you a Global Positioning System receiver to install in your vehicle. As part of your policy, it signals to the company how often, when, and on which highways you drive, and into which neighborhoods. The premium you pay reflects your actual driving risk rather than statistical averages of the entire population. If you drive a lot at night in high-risk areas, your premium will increase. If you drive in safe areas during the day, you'll pay less.

Five Massachusetts nanotech start-ups, including leaders MicroTubes and T³ (for Teeny Tiny Technology), announced they will pool portions of their equity into a single public offering coming to market under the

name NanoMech. Nanotechnology (microscopic-size machinery) prom-
ises to be a multibillion-dollar industry, but no firm has broken out with
a successful product. T³ built an early nanomanipulator prototype for
immersible scrubbers, microscopic cleansers that do their work while
floating in liquids as diverse as gasoline and blood. Raising capital has
been difficult, and none of the five companies is ready to go public on its
own. Nor are they sharing secrets. "We're competitors, not a consor-
tium," said Fred Wells, founder and president of T³, of Stoughton,
Massachusetts, one of the five companies involved. "This offer is a risk
diversification strategy for both the companies and their investor."

A woman sued for divorce on the grounds of adultery, charging that her
husband had engaged in sex over the Internet with a woman he never met.

WHICH OF THESE THREE STORIES are true? Can you tell fact
from fiction? All three, after all, illustrate a world in which we can
measure risks and create new financial securities that allow parties
to trade them.

The insurance company is offering a way for policyholders to
seize an opportunity from the jaws of high-cost auto insurance, by
measuring your risk as you drive and incorporating the measurement into the financial contract by which you lay off your risk for a
fee—your insurance policy. You pay only for the risk you consume.

The nanotech companies are applying risk management principles to private equities. They are going public as a group to reduce
the risk that they'll run out of cash before they hit it big. The "con-
sortium" is creating a new security by pooling the risks of each company, offering investors a pure play in nanotech, minimizing the risk
of betting on the wrong management team. This is not without
precedent. When Steve Jobs founded Apple, for example, he and a
friend who was also starting a technology company swapped 5 percent of their founder's stock, so each would have twice the chance
of financial success—and half the risk of total failure.[1]

In the cybersex story, the wife is claiming that virtual is as good (or bad) as real. Are thoughts the same as acts? Are verbal acts a valid surrogate for physical acts? If they are for the errant husband, then why not so for the aggrieved wife? Jimmy Carter famously lusted in his heart, and Clinton did so physically in the Oval Office. What will we say about transgressions that lie somewhere in between, in the electronic ether?

Each story illustrates the connected economy's effect on risk. The insurance story is about real-sector connection: Observing your car electronically measures the physical risks you take. NanoMech is a financial connection, linking companies that are unconnected in the real world to create a less risky security (a pure play) risk that investors will prefer to any of the constituents.

The potential divorce has financial consequences. The connected economy has progressed to the point that, in addition to changing businesses and markets, it is fueling new forces in the economy. Three are of particular importance.

First, information has become so rich and easily available that the market for risk has become hellishly efficient. Drive faster, pay more.

Second, the decline of the physical as a basis for value has underscored human talent and intellectual capital as the scarcest resources for creating wealth. You can sell the idea of nanotech before it becomes a commercial reality.

Third, the growing debates over copyright, cryptography, and privacy laws signal the growing mismatch between social capital developed in the industrial era and in the connected economy. Is it possible for two people to commit adultery without physically meeting?

These three forces are driving future wealth.

EFFICIENT MARKETS FOR EVERYTHING

Efficient markets are central to the way economic wealth is valued and traded. Connectivity is increasing efficiency by eliminating intermediaries between buyers and sellers and allowing them to find each other, negotiate, and trade more easily. Individuals making their own e-trades do so for as little as $4.96, for example, compared to the hundreds of dollars a few years ago.[2] This kind of stock trading over the Internet now accounts for more than 20 percent of all volume.[3]

To be "efficient," markets must be transparent, liquid, adjust continually, and offer open access.

Transparent markets present all information relevant to a transaction cheaply, immediately, and symmetrically to all parties. Market information used to be asymmetric—sellers generally had more information than buyers about any transaction, be it stocks, automobiles, or real estate. In the connected economy, transparent markets put all players on a more equal footing. Day traders can see the New York Stock Exchange (NYSE) floor specialist. The Internet enables savvy buyers to collect all kinds of information on products and services, including consumer reports, peer reviews, competitive prices. Multiple listings and 3-D virtual tours are increasing buyers' abilities to choose houses thousands of miles away.

Liquidity means that an investor's position can easily be sold out without affecting the market price materially. The easier and less expensive it is to switch into cash, the more liquid the asset. This used to imply a large number of buyers and sellers. But that's changing. For example, eBay, the on-line auction site, is in the business of making the illiquid flow. By accessing the marketplace's supply and demand, eBay enables a buyer to be found for the outgrown bicycle or used musical instrument at a price that makes it worth selling—a true secondary market.

Continuous adjustment of price is the third sign of efficient markets. How often does your company change the prices of its products and services? In an efficient market, buyers and sellers are continually adjusting the price to clear the market. Imagine the price of coffee in supermarkets being tied to commodity futures and weather reports and changing continuously, as lobster prices do on restaurant menus. You already see the thin edge of this particular wedge on eBay and at the gasoline pump, where prices often change daily.

As efficient markets become easy to establish on-line, they are *open to more people*, the fourth characteristic. Increasingly, trading is open to everybody, from the biggest company to the individual sitting at home with a PC. Witness the extraordinary growth in on-line brokerages and e-traders and the buyers and sellers who strike deals via eBay. Beyond securities, start-ups such as Mercata and accompany.com are organizing customer demand and presenting it to the market, improving symmetry between buyers and sellers of everything, both real and financial.

Efficient markets have been pioneered in finance, but the Net also brings market efficiency to the real economy. Web sites enable buyers and sellers to find and qualify each other and to arrange payment. Next, they develop rating and certification capabilities. As a consequence, all kinds of markets for products, services, and financial instruments that used to be closed within corporate boundaries are becoming open markets that are more competitive, faster to reflect new conditions, and more accessible—in short, more efficient.

Anything you can sell today, you can auction today. Airline seats (priceline.com), collectibles of every sort (eBay.com), telecommunications capacity (Band-X.com), industrial components (Fast-Parts.com), professionals' services (bid4geeks.com)—the efficient market model is spreading faster than an auctioneer can talk. Of course, medical ethics bump into the free markets of the Internet, as can be seen from the real but illegal attempt on eBay to auction a healthy kidney. eBay stopped the auction, but not before the top offer reached $5.7 million.[4]

In the financial world, anything you can sell or buy tomorrow, you can negotiate terms for today, called a *futures contract*. Futures markets arose from the real side of the economy, where a contract for future delivery could be an important reducer of risk. For example, Red Lobster could assure itself that it will receive a steady supply of shrimp at a known price throughout, say, the next twelve months, making it easier to price meals.

And once a market exists for these contracts, so does the opportunity to bet on the price movement of the underlying rubber, oil, pork bellies, or caviar—in principle, anything that can be sufficiently defined to trade through a standardized "option" contract. The future price of anything can become the basis of a bet. When the bet itself can be readily traded, it's said to be "securitized" just like a stock or bond. And once a risk is securitized, financial markets can invent new ways for people to trade their risks.

Before the futures markets arose, if you wanted to hedge your risk, you needed to actually own the commodity you were concerned about. Now you can hedge just about any real risk, through special-purpose financial instruments, which we'll discuss in chapter 5. As a consequence, you can trade options on an ever-wider set of financial bets.

Investment banks deftly find twice, thrice, and four-times-removed opportunities to trade risk through complex hedges, options, and other derivatives. Global corporations use the same instruments to trade not only their goods and services, but also the risks of currencies, commodity prices, and even the weather. Even communities are getting into the act. As the highest point in many towns, for example, church steeples now have value to wireless providers. Sometime soon, some enterprising church will auction off the option to use its steeple.

We can expect markets as efficient as the capital markets, not only for financial instruments, but for everything. Time-shared airplane space, baseball cards, time in famed cardiologist Denton Cooley's operating schedule, eggs from 5'10" Radcliffe graduates (eggdonor.com). Once these markets are established, futures, derivatives, hedges, and all the rest will follow.

PRIMACY OF HUMAN CAPITAL

A beautiful woman once approached Pablo Picasso in a Paris café. She asked him to sketch her and offered to pay him fair value. In a few minutes, the artist created a drawing—and asked for 500,000 francs.
"But it only took you a few minutes," the tourist protested.
"No," Picasso supposedly replied, "it took me about 40 years."

Picasso valued his human capital, not his labor. The cliché is becoming the reality. In the agrarian world, landowners valued people pretty much as farm animals. In the industrial world, captains of industry valued people for their skills as part of the machine. In the connected economy, we value people for their knowledge and talent. And as software automates the traditional work of people, human capital will become the scarce resource in business. That's why business has declared a "war for talent." Competitive advantage depends on attracting and keeping stronger talent better than the other guy.

The Picasso principle applies to countless non-artists—surgeons, pilots, and scientists among them. Their value represents the sum of their experience, skills, and potential, adjusted for the scarcity of their talents and the demands for them. You're no different. All you know, all you've done, all your contacts and relationships, and the intelligence you bring to future work give you a value in the marketplace—albeit not yet an efficient one.

When land was the productive asset, nations battled over it. The same is happening now in a global war for talented people. When Singapore embarked on its "intelligent island" strategy in 1980, its Economic Development Board concluded that the nation lacked the human capital necessary to execute the strategy. Singapore then contacted all expatriates who had left to develop their human capital abroad and enticed them handsomely to return.[5]

Not all human capital must relocate to find its market. Indian and Welsh software writers, for example, are thriving due to global demand for their skills and readily available connectivity. Russian animators hold meetings over the Net with their Hollywood customers and bargain successfully for fees that approach world scale. By contrast, Russian musicians, who can trade their human capital only locally, are going begging—literally.

At the end of the twentieth century, businesses spent hundreds of millions setting up sophisticated cost systems for every conceivable type of asset but one: human capital. As the scarcity of the precious asset becomes more obvious, we will come to rely on the markets—our most reliable source—to do the valuation for us. As we'll see, the owners of human capital—individuals—will be calling the tune. Remember, you can pay for labor hours, but your staff Picassos will take their sketches elsewhere.

OBSOLESCENCE OF SOCIAL CAPITAL

American society believes deeply that creating economic wealth requires political freedom. Freedom without order leads to chaos. Order without freedom is totalitarian. The two are always married, always at odds.

In the seventeenth century, Thomas Hobbes and John Locke argued over the tensions between self-interest and communal need, and between economic affairs and social purpose. They sparked debate among America's founders, pitting Thomas Jefferson's declaration of individual liberty and the pursuit of happiness against John Adams' emphasis on community and order.

In the twentieth century, the economic debate bounced between market mechanisms and planned economies. Do you need political freedoms for free markets to thrive? Do markets do better when governments keep their hands off? Or does unbridled capitalism destroy community? From Teddy Roosevelt in the United States to Margaret Thatcher in the United Kingdom, and from Lenin in Russia to Deng Xiaoping in China, leaders and nations have argued these two sides eloquently.

The infrastructure shift to the connected economy is raising anew the perennial tensions between freedom and order. The cost of freedom is that communication networks spread computer viruses and hate mail, raise questions of privacy, and allow people to publish bomb-making instructions from anywhere in the world. But the benefits include the freedom to exchange tremendous amounts of valuable information, not least the numbers that permit financial markets to operate globally. Now legislators debate about copyright, free speech, child pornography, and the ownership and export of encryption technology.

These developments are only the most superficial sign that our social institutions are obsolete. As the half-life of knowledge shrinks, our attitudes toward public and corporate education will change, so our educational institutions, public and private, will need an overhaul as their technologies change and then output measurements become explicit. Similarly, extended age spans, birth control, and greater economic opportunity for women are radically altering the role of the family.[6] Our social capital is wearing out. We need a new generation of solutions.

These three forces—the growing efficiency of financial and real markets, the primacy of human capital, and the obsolescence of social capital—all result from the developing connected economy. Efficient markets are a direct result of the greater connectivity provided by the Net. The primacy of human capital is to a great extent the outcome of software's becoming smart enough to automate the traditional roles of people in business. The obsolescence of our social capital is a consequence of technology's impact on our privacy, security, and property rights. All three drivers intermingle with one another and, as we shall now see, lead the way to the three themes of future wealth.

Oh, by the way: We made up NanoMech, though it's been endorsed conceptually by investment bankers. The other two examples are real.[7]

3

FROM BARTER
TO BLOOMBERG
Trading Risk and Human Capital

In 1626, Native Americans traded Manhattan to Peter Minuit, director general of the Dutch colony of New Netherlands, for a bunch of trinkets and beads later valued at about $24.

Through your Bloomberg home financial terminal (mybloomberg.com), you just sold your Manhattan coop for $1 million and rolled the money into your daughter's IPO. The display showed a large increase in your portfolio's risk position, and a reduction of thirteen months in your likely retirement age. A red dialogue box appears, alerting you that the chance of personal bankruptcy has risen above your threshold level of 1 in 1,000.

FOR MOST PEOPLE, risk is a four-letter word, whether we're speaking of floods, earthquakes, car crashes, or viruses. The real world is chock-full of such risks. In the financial world, tolerance for risk can create opportunity, as in the two examples above. As long as you can afford to lose part of the time, risk is attractive. And the higher the return you seek, the higher the risk you'll need to run. These ideas are fundamental to the capital asset pricing model (CAPM), developed by Nobel Prize winner William Sharpe, on which most of modern finance is founded.[1] CAPM makes a simple assumption: that an investor will not take more risk—defined as the uncertainty of the outcome times potential loss—without gaining extra reward. Empirically, this proves true for investors choosing between blue chips and derivatives, or gamblers at the track choosing daily doubles and trifectas. Investors don't want risk for its own sake, though gamblers and thrill seekers do. Rather, they want to take all the risk they can prudently afford, to maximize their expected future worth.

RISK AS OPPORTUNITY

If you can afford to lose, high-risk investments will make you more money. Think junk bonds, LBOs, and Internet IPOs, all of which offer potentially great returns for those with the wherewithal to ride out the ups and downs. In contrast, when everyone worked in dangerous factories, risk involved life-or-death outcomes—no one could afford to lose.

In a bull market, risk involves modest or magnificent outcomes, The more we take, the greater our potential gains. The recent performance of the U.S. market, according to former U.S. Secretary of the Treasury Robert Rubin at the 1999 World Economic Forum, has us as a nation "reaching for yield," seeking more risk because our expectations are increasing.[2] Of course, the bull market's end will affect these attitudes—at least temporarily.

Any risk whose uncertainty is reasonably measurable can be the basis of a financial instrument, and therefore traded. While stocks and bonds are the staple instruments, others include insurance, options, hedges, and many more financial arcana, many of which are designed to offer higher risk. As we become more affluent or confident, we seek these higher yields, and the financial industry presents more high-risk opportunities in affordable packages. We are discovering how to measure more uncertainties, such as the odds of making a hit movie, finding oil, or winning FDA approval for a new drug. Once investors accumulate statistics on the conditions and outcomes of such risks, they can become the basis for new securities.

Everything of value has risk attached to it, upside and downside. In the real world, we tend to think about the downside of assets— car theft, house fire. We lay off these problems through *insurance*, a financial instrument that makes our risk return trade-off more to our liking. And we sell this risk to insurance companies that profit by bearing pools of such risks. Upside risk is the chance that an asset will appreciate, an opportunity we address through *investment*. When you buy a stock, you think the upside risk is a better deal than a guaranteed rate on a safer T-bill. The upper class invests, the working class insures, the middle class does some of each. Should the middle-class family that inherits some extra money reduce its volatility—risk—by paying off its mortgage? Or increase both its upside and downside risk by buying a hot Internet stock?

In the world of future wealth, attitudes are shifting toward risk as opportunity. In both real and financial cases, we trade risks, but in opposite directions: almost always reducing the risk from the real and increasing the risk from the financial, ideally for a larger overall return. In both cases, we pay a financial institution for its role in the trade.

This risk trading is not only about investments and finance. After decades of lip service to "taking chances," corporate managers are being rewarded for taking more business risk. The ability to successfully choose the risks worth bearing is a form of human capital, whether based on long experience or on acute judgment. The elevated returns from higher risk represent a return on this human capital.

With real assets, the more downside risk protection you practice, the more you limit potential *problems*. With financial assets, the more risk protection you practice, the more you limit potential *opportunities*. You may also limit downside risk, as when you liquidate stocks to buy an annuity. In both cases, insurance and investment, the best solution depends on both what you can afford to lose and your tolerance for volatility.

We have always dealt with downside risk. Early interpreters of signs, whether in cards, bones, or numbers, have always sought to predict the future. How can we know the will of the gods and protect ourselves against unknowable disasters? In both mathematics and economics, this problem evolved into probability theory, the measurable likelihood of events. Laws of probability are based on what happens over large numbers of instances of situations we cannot control—a 16 percent chance of rolling a seven, a fifty-fifty likelihood of rain, the 8:1 odds on a horse.[3]

Probability nonetheless brought us a kind of long-term certainty and with it a sense of the inevitable. By contrast, uncertainty has a sense of the possible. The one speaks of control, the other of freedom. Treating risk as a measurable uncertainty, rather than as a probability, frees us. As Peter L. Bernstein concludes in *Against the Gods*, the great risk analysts "transformed the perception of risk from chance of loss into opportunity for gain, from fate and original design to sophisticated, probability-based forecasts of the future, and from helplessness to choice."[4]

Society as a whole is now following this path. As the middle class accumulates financial assets more rapidly than real assets, it is learning a new approach to wealth accumulation. The pensions of the proverbial widows and orphans are no longer invested in bonds of public utilities. Rather, retirees own shares in various mutual funds and can trade in and out of these funds. And some very high-risk, high-reward assets, like the Picasso drawing, are real, not financial.

We can also adjust the financial risk in our lives through our decisions on real risk in health care, pensions, and insurance, and the number of vehicles for managing risk will only increase. Instead of the real sector's setting standards and dictating behavior for the financial one, the financial rules the real. As divorce lawyers say: The real united them, the financial split them.

The rich man's approach, diversify and seek risk, is replacing the poor man's approach, put your eggs into one basket and trade the risk away. The former puts money in mutual funds, the latter puts money in life insurance. Such financial wealth results partly from shifting the basis of commerce from low-risk/low-return lending, the historical dominion of banks, to high-risk/high-return investing—where bankers now want to be allowed to operate.

> *An article in the* U.S. Journal of Medicine *reports that people with the Fj3 factor on chromosome 15 have the lowest cancer rates in the population. "They are immune to many of the oncogenetic factors that affect the rest of us," says Dr. Mohan Samtani, leader of the research group. When Betty Ryder's Internet clipping service reads her the news, she pulls up her husband, Bob's, Personal Genome Record and determines that he is indeed one of the lucky few. After a celebration dinner that night, the Ryders waste no time logging onto eSchwab.com, where they redirect their investment portfolio. Knowing Bob will likely be around longer than they had thought, they shift their mix to higher-risk/higher-yield securities. The next day, the insurance company e-mails them to confirm that the premium on Bob's major medical policy has been reduced.*

DEVELOPING FINANCIAL MARKETS FOR HUMAN CAPITAL

In the venture community today, money is everywhere, and brains are scarce. Capital markets value scarcity—they are our means of allocating scarce resources—so they will learn to put a value on intellectual capital. As the financial markets begin to create a price for people, ways to trade human capital will develop and blend into the global risk market, just like gold futures. Someday soon, molecular biologists could indeed be up 3 points and economists down ¼.

eBay, the on-line Internet auction house, foreshadows this market. Only four years old, with a payroll of just 140 people, it is "the fastest-growing retailer in the history of the universe," according to Morgan Stanley's star Internet analyst Mary Meeker. Log on to <www.eBay.com> and bid on almost anything, from golf clubs to lessons with a golf pro.[5] On April 28, 1999, even eBay seemed to outdo itself when Item #96369441 went up for bid:

> *Team of 16 employees from major ISP [Internet service provider] willing to leave as a group. 1 Director ($200K) 2 Managers ($180K) 3 Senior Engineers ($190K) 5 Administrators ($150K) Possibly more.*

The group cited its experience ("implemented major NT and UNIX web presence" for Fortune 500 clients) and then noted that, with one-year salary needs, a signing bonus ($320,000), 401(k) and stock option plans, the total minimum bid for their services was $3.14 million.

The audacious item represents some sort of watershed. The team used an auction to create a market value for its brains. The team members offered themselves, or more accurately a bundle of their brains and skills, participating with the buyer in the risk and reward of the exchange. No one bid, and the attempt failed, but the idea had made its mark.

Others followed. Less than a month later, John Kinsella, one of the original 16 employees of eBay, created bid4geeks.com, a Web site for individuals or teams of workers to measure the market value of their human capital. Kinsella sees his site as a valuable tool for the large numbers of "people in high tech who have no idea what they are worth."[6] Monster.com followed on Independence Day with a job auction site, Talent Market (<talentmarket.Monster.com>), and reported 100,000 registered contractors within two months of launch and 26,500 auctions by November 1999—though actual transactions have been slow to materialize.[7]

Electronic markets, with offers bid and asked, will likely challenge headhunters and help-wanted ads in clearing the job markets. After this early phase rationalizes the familiar buy-sell exchanges called "hiring," then "contracting," "freelancing," and "outsourcing" innovations will slowly move the market for human capital into other financial instruments.

The next step could be futures. One of us recently took an option on the first slot in the spring calendar of a landscape contractor—$1,000 down payment to be credited against the bill or forfeited if the work were awarded to someone else—a service future. That was a face-to-face transaction, but over time, *job markets will morph into human capital markets*, trading a variety of wealth-creating activities from job creation and placement to rationing scarce talent.

Today the market for human capital is one of the least efficient in our economy. As the connected economy trend of competitive information and on-line markets continues, however, the inevitable outcome will be global, efficient markets for human capital.

Dr. Deborah Fields, the great granddaughter of Jonas Salk, and 347 other highly regarded scientists received a letter from the Wellcome Foundation, inviting them to participate in the GenomicGeniuses Fund. The foundation represents the major pharmaceutical firms that a few years earlier completed the map of the human genome. The letter says in part, "our knowledge is among the world's most productive assets. By turning your most valuable asset, your talent and capability, into a pooled and tradable security, you will lower your individual risk and participate in expected superior returns." Although she is oriented to science, not investments, Dr. Fields did turn next to the catalogue for yachts under 100 feet that had arrived in the same day's mail.

HIGHER WIRES, STRONGER NETS

In pursuit of their desires, individuals and companies assume greater risk, working on higher wires, with greater potential for fall and injury. The financial markets are packaging higher risks in smaller units, so that a broader range of investors can participate. Putnam Investments, Thomas H. Lee Co., J&W Seligman, and Pilgrim Baxter, for example, have introduced private equity funds, pooling what used to be single $2 to $20 million investments and dividing them into chunks of as little as $250,000.[8]

What is true for individuals and companies is also true for nations. The United States is an extreme of economic Darwinism which tends to let the fittest businesses survive or die with little government intervention. At the same time, however, the SEC sets rules of eligibility to protect yield-hungry investors from taking risks they can't afford, and the bankruptcy laws offer some protection to those who lose too much. This social infrastructure (as well as many other kinds) is essential to the wealth-creating process in risk markets. Russia's attempts to introduce capitalism without this infrastructure have caused its people's standard of living to plummet.

Whether societies build sufficient safety nets to save those who assume great risk, yet fail, stands to be one of the dominant legislative and social issues of the next twenty years. And it's also likely to be one of the leading determinants of future national bounty. Simply put, *societies that best support risk taking—high wires, strong nets—rather than limiting risk taking to ensure security will create the greatest innovation and growth,* as bankruptcy laws have done in the past. Such societies also support the greatest social mobility.

Too much freedom is exhilarating but also frightening. Too much order is comforting to many but also stultifying. Sometimes one ascends, sometimes the other.

Creating such institutions is challenging. A net that rescues failures indiscriminately creates what economists call "moral hazard"—

the temptation to take large risks without precedent because society will give you a financial mulligan. Finding the right balance will consume a lot of legislative and judicial resources. The economic outcomes of the twentieth century show us that some forms of order—such as a trustworthy system of contract law and the ability to enforce accountability—are essential to economic progress.

Through the 1990s, the U.S. economy thrived as new options proliferated. On-line gambling, electronic day trading, access to unregulated high-risk investments, and, above all, lower-risk entrepreneurship are all examples of new freedoms. Congress has just repealed the laws that restricted freedoms of certain financial institutions. Attempts to reassert order include a public encryption standard with the keys held by the federal government, movements to restrict biotechnology research, and restrictions on exporting encryption software. These have been rejected.

The connected economy will favor freedom over constraint. Some forms of regulation—child labor laws or occupational safety, say—promote social goals and wealth. But detailed prescriptions—who should do what job, dictated by a supreme Soviet or by a union contract—stifle innovation and initiative. As all risks become tradable and outcomes become transparent and controllable not through rules but through consequences, what goes around actually will come around. Bankruptcy laws are a long-standing and successful example. The development of a safety net that encourages risk taking without guaranteeing a bailout will be a social and legal challenge for the twenty-first century. We are searching for freedom with order, the so-called edge of chaos.

Convicted virus writer and hacker Alan Shannon was paroled from Walla Walla Prison after serving four years of his seven-year sentence. Terms of his parole stated that all his electronic communications for the rest of his life must display the following warning: "The Internet General has determined that communications from this individual may be dangerous to your information system, and cause data loss, system damage, or both." This was another application of the electronic watermark system, first developed to authenticate financial transfers and later used to control distribution of pirated music and pornography. The ACLU immediately filed a suit challenging the ruling's constitutionality. "Information wants to be free" banners reappeared everywhere, and Shannon tattooed a ball and chain on his forehead to symbolize the burden he would bear.

"They've gone about this the wrong way," said Citigroup's Robert Rubin, former secretary of the treasury. "Shannon should be made to pay for liability insurance covering anyone whose information he damages."

These, then, are the three themes of *Future Wealth* (see the figure "Dynamics of Future Wealth"):

Risk as Opportunity. There is opportunity to trade upside and downside risk in every asset, real and financial. Higher risk yields higher return—on average. The connected economy makes information about assets and their futures available to everyone, so every asset will come to support a financial instrument that can be traded, hedged, or optioned. A growing number of middle-class people will trade many kinds of risks through the financial markets to achieve the upside and downside exposures that make them most comfortable.

Financial Markets for Human Capital. As all markets become efficient and human capital moves center stage, it is inevitable that financial markets will develop for all forms of human capital, from people's time and labor (bid4geeks) to their heritage (why not put the right to auction your estate jewelry up for bids?). Along the way, expect serious ethical issues (there are already auctions for women's eggs). Efficient markets allow us to slide easily between the real and the financial.

Higher Wires, Stronger Nets. The connected economy has created great opportunities to take risk. If enough bubbles burst, there will be a reaction to restrict risk taking. Regardless, we will need new limits and guidelines, ethical and legal constraints. The connected economy has given us new freedoms and opportunities. Just as surely, it will require new means to provide selective forms of security for those who fall off the high wire.

All three themes will create radical changes in wealth, as the connected economy has already transformed production. In the next three parts, we'll look in turn at individuals, companies, and society as a whole to see how these things will rearrange our lives.

PART II

individuals

ONCE WE SEE OUR TALENT—athletic, intellectual, charismatic—as a kind of productive economic unit, we'll be able to reconsider what kind of capital structure we can make of and for ourselves. Some entertainers and sports figures have already issued personal securities. Personal capital structures of some kind will become commonplace, and soon thereafter you'll be able to trade, securitize, and diversify your intellectual capital position. The degree of risk you take—and how much of it you lay off to others—will be your call.

The biggest hurdle between you and future wealth is mind-set: You must believe that your most valuable assets are your own experience, smarts, and potential. And you must be prepared to risk it. The biggest risk of all? That you play it too safe.

FROM PAYCHECK TO PORTFOLIO
Know Thy Worth

Michael Jordan's Restaurant will soon be Sammy Sosa's. The owners say they're turning Jordan's restaurant in Chicago to Sammy Sosa's Restaurant by the opening of next baseball season. They say Jordan's place remains profitable, but its popularity is slipping. As for Sosa, they say, the Cubs star will be required to make appearances at the renamed establishment. Jordan's restaurant will move to a smaller location.[1]

"KNOW THY WORTH." Great advice for individuals who want to flourish in the world of future wealth—a world in which you must change from spectator to player. The cash flows to Jordan and Sosa weren't published, but theirs is a clear case of "basketball players off in light trading." In today's economy, playing means leveraging your smarts. Increasingly, individuals will create future wealth by marketing what they know. Instead of producing objects and ideas for others, they'll do so for themselves. This human capital lies in everything that people do well, be it an athlete's speed, an entrepreneur's self-confidence, or a software writer's imagination. It is the intangible age's equivalent to the factories of the industrial era or the family farm of the agricultural society. We have met the productive capacity of the information economy, and it is us.

Consider two premises of the connected economy. First, financial markets will underwrite future performance and learn to do so ever more efficiently. Second, creating future value depends more and more on people's brains and talents. Together, financial markets will underwrite people's future performance.

As human capital becomes the basis for future wealth, the reach and appetite of the market for it will grow, and the degree of tolerable risk will increase. Hocking your head will become as common as mortgaging your mansion. Once this happens, trading the financial instruments that back individuals—not unlike trading mortgage-backed securities—will follow.

VALUING HUMAN CAPITAL

For more than two centuries, inventors have collected fees from patents, and authors, royalties from literary works. What has changed is the treatment of intangible value. Henry Bessemer invented the steel-making process, and Andrew Carnegie built U.S. Steel. Unlike Carnegie, however, Bessemer never achieved great wealth. His intellectual property was counted as only a minor part of Carnegie's company.

Netscape's cofounder, Marc Andreessen, by contrast, became one of fiction writer Neal Stephenson's "software khans."[2] In the information age, it doesn't take a steel mill to put your idea in the marketplace. Andreessen had the imagination and the skill to move first with the browser. Now that Wall Street understands the inventive value of Andreessen, it will invest an enormous amount in him. Jerry Yang and David Filo, who created the first Web directory while they were undergraduates at Stanford University, founded Yahoo! and are now each in possession of tens of billions of dollars worth of paper.[3]

These days, people with good track records can even collect money up front, before they do the next thing. Jim Clark (founder of Silicon Graphics, Netscape, and Healtheon) gets paid big pieces of equity for contributing a business concept. A brilliant engineer collects a fat signing bonus when he joins a firm, Stephen King collects huge advances on novels he may not even start writing for years, and first-draft choices, such as the Colts' Payton Manning, have millions in the bank before their rookie season opens. The talented product designer will want a share of every project. Phillippe Starck and Adam Tihany, just like movie stars, will want a share of the gross of the hotels and restaurants they design. Once that happens, they will have income streams, which in turn could back securities that can be traded. And why not? Many Internet IPOs rest on little more than the reputations of their board members.

MIGRATION OF HUMAN CAPITAL

More companies are accepting that their biggest assets leave the building and go home every night. So why shouldn't they act like Elvis? What has long been common in sectors like entertainment, publishing, and investment banking is now spreading through all industries. Talent migrates, and value travels with it.

Meanwhile, the migration of intellectual capital has accelerated from a trickle to a torrent. In the United States, restructuring and outsourcing created massive layoffs in the eighties, effectively bursting huge dams of human capital. Many came to recognize that their personal crisis in fact represented an opportunity. They began to work as independent contractors, built their personal brands, and let the market determine their value. As this trend continues, we will come to see employment in a different light.

The industrial company operated as if labor were another factory part. Men were interchangeable; they turned a wrench every seventeen seconds. This interchangeability made the labor market a buyer's market: Here's the job, take it or leave it. Even when organized labor helped to balance power, union members were a commodity differentiated by seniority, not capability.

The markets of the connected economy are too impatient, too well informed, and too greedy to treat "labor" that way. They seek talent relentlessly and match it to its most productive use. And, of course, the tasks have changed as the economy has grown intangible. So, for example, from 1995 to 1999, companies paid big premiums for SAP programmers, and seasoned CEOs in Silicon Valley now work for themselves, advising multiple start-ups. The market is finding ways to provide talent with returns commensurate with their abilities. Add connectivity, and you've explained the burgeoning electronic marketplace for talent.

In 1999, the Web housed approximately 500 résumé clearinghouses, more than 100,000 companies posting job-related information opportunities, more than 2.5 million résumés, and at least 28,500 job boards, such as Monster.com, HotJobs.com, and CareerMosaic. com.[4] All of these sites help clear the job market more efficiently. They get a lot of help from networked communities like PlanetAll, a free web service that puts friends of friends together, and Guru.com, which enables independent professionals to book work.

TAKE BACK THE WEALTH

Individuals will come to see the labor market as controllable because they, and not their would-be employers, hold the desired resource. For now, businesses are constrained by the talent they have, whereas the talent is becoming free to go anywhere—electronically or physically.

To exercise this degree of freedom will mean a long workout on the big psychological StairMaster for most of us. First, you must compare your employment opportunities and economic rewards in terms of wealth rather than income. Second, you must realize that how you invest your human capital matters as much as how you invest your financial capital, for the same reason. Its rate of return determines your range of future options. Take a job for what it teaches you—for how much it will improve your skills, talents, and smarts—rather than for what it pays. And take it for the expanded set of options it will create. Go for appreciation and wealth, not consumption and income.

It's not hard to see how this changes the job interview or, indeed, who's really interviewing whom. Instead of a potential employer's asking, "Where do you see yourself in five years?" you'll ask, "If I invest my mental assets with you for five years, then how much will they appreciate? How much will my portfolio of options—career diversification, for example—grow? How do you intend to maximize my talent? With what star talent on staff will I work?" And you should demand nonevasive replies—maybe even a nonexclusive contract.

The fastest-growing segment of employment in the United States is self-employment. This means that, voluntarily or otherwise, more individuals are beginning to see their work lives not as jobs, but as a series of risk management choices.

Before automobiles, who valued black ooze in one's well? A horse needed water, not oil. Before risk markets, a family needed a paycheck. Most workers had few other options. But times change. Now anybody would love to find oil on his or her property. Today, we must plumb the value of our own natural resource, our human capital. One last point: If you found oil, would you start an oil company? Probably not. You'd sell rights to exploit what you owned. *Future Wealth* invites you to do the same with your human capital.

People who can afford multiple houses see their real estate this way—they consider its likelihood of appreciation and the market value of making improvements. The big switch is to see our human capital assets as a kind of private property. We own it, we can improve it, we can let it run down. And the "neighborhood" can change, reducing the value of your property, as it has for millions of factory workers as the economy shifted to the intangible.

Future Wealth Expectation: *People will still add economic value by using their human capital, but they'll maximize their wealth by trading it.*

5

FROM CORPORATE COG TO MARKET CAP

Maximizing the Value of Your Human Capital

With the Dow and Nasdaq hitting record highs seemingly every other day, I have decided, after discussing it with my wife and exercising the proxy of our newborn son, to take my family public. Since making the decision, I've had the most dizzying week. On Sunday night—before my wife and I had even gone to our board (of which we are the only two members) to get approval for the public offering—Goldman, Sachs called to say it was extremely interested in underwriting the IPO. It had crunched some numbers and looked at the multiples that comparable start-ups were getting. It said the Postman Family would probably go out at $12 to $14 per share on the first day of trading and hit $100 by day's end, before splitting 2 or even 3 for 1.

On Monday, Kleiner Perkins Caufield & Byers, Silicon Valley's top

venture capital firm, faxed me a proposal to seed the Postman Family
with $10 million for a 20 percent equity stake, and I accepted, though I
felt like a fool after lunch, when I got an offer of $20 mil for 10 percent.

—ANDREW POSTMAN[1]

NOT LONG AGO the entire financial industry saw that it could
securitize not only the debt of corporations and governments, but
also any debt backed by a predictable revenue stream—maybe even
the Postman family.

A single investment—in the mortgage of a home, for example—
is risky. In aggregate, however, the proportion of mortgages that will
be paid back is statistically predictable. Lenders therefore pool individual mortgages, just as insurance companies pool home policies:
to predict and manage default risk. This pool of lending risk can also
be securitized. Just like corporate debt, it can be packaged and sold
to investors. If you bundle a thousand $200,000 mortgages inside a
financial wrapper, then you can sell a $200 million mortgage-backed
security to the public and trade the risks. The banks earn a higher
rate of return on their investment because they can lend the same
money more often—selling the outstanding loans to other investors
and relending the proceeds of the sale, through a new mortgage, to
someone else. The financial markets get a new investment vehicle.
And individual borrowers get access to more capital, because the
mortgage banker is tapping additional sources of funds. Everybody's
happy.

If a bundle of home mortgages can be securitized, why not a
bundle of car loans? Or business loans? Or machine leases, shut-
tered power plants, tax liens, and bad debts? Sure enough, securitization wraps its way around assets that evaporate, such as unused
airline tickets, and spreads into products not yet made, such as
movies. This was true of everything except for people. Then along
came David Bowie.

SECURITIZING HUMAN CAPITAL

With his business manager, the Pullman Group, and a New York investment bank, the British rock star issued $55 million in 15-year Bowie Bonds. Moody's Investor Service promptly awarded the notes "Single A," putting them on a par with General Motors. Prudential Insurance Company of America snapped up the entire offering.[2]

Bonds come in all shapes and sizes, of course, ranging from the dull and safe (like municipal debt and the low interest earned on those bonds) to the sexier, but higher risk (like leveraged buyouts and the high-interest junk bonds that finance them). Measured by 7.9 percent annual interest yield—only 20 basis points more than a comparable corporate bond—Bowie's landed comfortably in the safe zone.

The respectability of Bowie Bonds stems directly from what secures them, namely future royalties earned by the 300 or so tracks that Bowie has written and recorded over the years, plus his earnings from future concert tours. Bowie is clearly no space cadet when planning his future wealth. He, not his publisher, owns the rights to virtually every track of his 25 albums included in this deal, a critical factor maximizing Bowie's future wealth. Bowie has done an exceptional job of retaining his human capital and evaluating his options to invest in it, brand it, and license it. "He wanted to lease out his babies. He didn't want to lose them forever," said Robert Sablowsky, a senior vice president at Fahnestock Inc., the former parent of the Pullman Group, the investment bank that created the deal. "He was offered more to sell them outright."[3] Few of us consider these options in contracting with our employers . . . so far.

In exchange for the interest he'll be paying and the lien against his future earnings, Bowie got the $55 million up front. But he's also trading risk. Rather than staying trapped with all his eggs in his own basket, he can diversify his investments and spread his risks, while holding on to the upside of his music.

The Pullman Group also helped other entertainers follow suit, demonstrating that this was not a one-time thing. In 1998, Edward and Brian Holland and Lamont Dozier, the creative brains behind the Motown label (their many hits include the Supremes' "Stop in the Name of Love") issued a $30 million bond.[4] Moody's gave it a "Single A" rating. The big difference here was that, as songwriters rather than performers, the income came from a pool of many different artists, which diversified the overall risk of the bond. In contrast, James Brown, the Godfather of Soul, collected $100 million with bonds secured by royalties from some 750 of his past recordings.[5]

These bonds reflect the risk that the market will bear. Sometimes risk scares all comers. Death Row Records, the hot label for gangsta-rap music, tried to float a $25 million bond with Nomura Securities, backed by recordings of three Death Row artists: Tupac Shakur, Snoop Doggy Dogg, and Dr. Dre.[6] But Tupac Shakur was murdered in Las Vegas the year before, and the two surviving rappers, along with Shakur's father, were contesting Death Row's ownership of the collateral rights. Needless to say, no collateral ownership, no buyers. *Musta got their goat/ the deal don' float/ Sunk down deep by a risk overcoat.*

Sports teams have also joined the race to raise cash from future income streams. Merrill Lynch helped Italy's Lazio soccer club raise $25 million against future ticket sales. The bank got another $50 million for the Real Madrid football club, secured by future revenues from Adidas' sponsorship of the team.[7]

What's new here? The people who floated bonds essentially offered going business concerns, similar to future income streams or guaranteed sponsorship deals from reputable corporations as collateral. Each had a reasonably predictable cash stream. Probably all of them—the individuals or the sports teams—could have borrowed the money from a bank on some terms. But issuing bonds likely netted them cheaper interest rates and gave them greater control and flexibility over the terms. It also transferred the risk from the talent to the buyer, from the lender to the investor. It got them media attention, just as important in a human capital–intense economy. Wouldn't you like a bond named after you?

THE GROWTH OF HUMAN CAPITAL SECURITIES

As more such securities emerge, the market for them will become ever more liquid. Moreover, the liquidity will fuel the spread of even more such bonds, as a greater variety of talented people securitize their own future wealth. Brace yourself.

No one has yet traded the securities mentioned above. Prudential, for instance, still holds its Bowies. When bonds—or shares, for that matter—aren't traded, they don't produce a market price; and so no one knows how deep or wide the interest in them really is. We will know, soon. A Japanese bank is trying to trade a portion of one such issue. Presumably, it will sell at some price, and the deal will make financial market history. Trading securities backed by human capital will make an investor's stake in an individual liquid, and liquidity is an essential catalyst for growth of a new market. After all, few will buy what they can't sell.

Some investors buy corporate bonds to hold. Others are more active traders. The rating agencies, such as Moody's and Standard & Poor's, continually assess the risks and publish their opinions— AAA, BAA, and so on—and the prices change in response. The flurry attracts investors of all stripes, ranging from conservative long-termers to flighty day traders, high on risk. The same people will swarm around personal bonds once liquidity frees that market.

Once investors get interested, as additional talent pools learn about efficient markets for human capital—theirs—the markets are sure to broaden. In the wake of professional stars, star professionals will auction their talents. In fact, that's already happening, as with the management team that advertised itself on eBay.

Once it begins, trade in human capital is sure to speed off in many directions. Imagine this: You've booked Tom Peters to speak at your big conference a year from now, for his customary five-figure fee. Michael Milken needs Peters for his Knowledge Universe conference the same day. No stranger to financial puzzles, Milken offers you $20,000 to assign Peters' future commitment to him. You realize that for the original fee plus Milken's offer you can get both Stan Davis and Chris Meyer with big money to spare. Peters is as unaffected as a pork belly traded on the Chicago exchange. And you've just traded human capital.

GETTING IN ON THE ACT

You don't have to be a rock-and-roll star, an athlete, or a motivational speaker to market your assets, because most of us possess the assets that investors want. Look around you. You have repeat customers, a huge Rolodex, and more ideas than you know what to do with. Your boss gives you bonuses and options. Your reputation prompts headhunters to call.

Pioneers see a safety in numbers, their odds of survival increase, and investors in human capital likely share that view. Remember how mortgages became less risky when bundled together in a financial wrapper? The same is true of professionals. Physicians unite to form a practice and easily find financial backers. You, too, can bundle your talent with that of your peers for greater future wealth.

How does a new Harvard MBA differ as a public offering from a single mortgage? Not much. Not every Harvard grad makes the grade. The stakes are too small, and the risk too great to make her marketable. What if the Harvard MBA class of 2001 bundled itself and turned its aggregate future earnings stream into a public offering? What if the Baker Scholars—the top 5 percent of the class—bundled themselves and went to market? One Baker Scholar in a hundred could come a cropper, so investors might shy from a single individual's bond. But we suspect that, as a group, Baker scholars would be rated AAA—practically an Internet IPO.

Future investors will always look for ways to separate the intellectual wheat from the chaff, talent from nontalent, winnowing and funneling, all to yield gilt-edged prospects. Down the road, any class of U.S. Supreme Court clerks will produce its share of modestly paid judges and public servants. But it will also produce a majority of lawyers who ascend to mid-six-figure salaries by their mid- to late thirties. Again, bundled talent appeals more to investors. From your individual point of view, you should gladly bundle yourself to spread your risk and benefit from the aggregate.

BEYOND BONDS AND OPTIONS

So far, we've discussed debt and service obligations issuing bonds backed by some form of past (existing songs) or future (revenue streams) human capital. Bowie's published songs, not his future creations, secured the debt. His deal resembles a homeowner's using a home to secure a mortgage. The homeowner retains the appreciation in the house's value. Likewise, Bowie keeps the upside as his musical babies mature. That's the world of bonds and debt.

Shares and equity differ greatly. When we buy stock, we buy a portion of a corporation's risk, both upside and downside. Suppose, for example, that an entertainer issued equity in the future earning streams of some facets of his human capital, rather than a debt issue. Would we then watch the price of his shares soar or crash with news of slumping sales of his performances?

In fact, you can already see the implications of such a stock market for the movie industry, if only virtually. At <www.hsx.com>, you'll find the Hollywood Stock Exchange (HSX), where users can buy and sell virtual securities in media properties. As of late July 1998, HSX had lured in over 112,000 registered individuals in 120 countries, trading in excess of 150 million virtual shares daily—and no real money changes hands. In early 1999, for example, comedian Mike Myers (MMYER) rose HSX$60 to HSX$2391, in anticipation of Myers' much-awaited *Austin Powers: The Spy Who Shagged Me* (AUST2).[8]

HSX is a game, not a financial market—a way for movie fans to express their interest in the subject. Unlike Bowie bonds, MMYER's price isn't directly related to *Austin Powers'* receipts. Could this game be played for real money? One creative player managed to sell his HSX portfolio on eBay for $1,000, monetizing his fantasy portfolio.

In some circles the game already is played for real money, though it isn't formally organized as a game. Golfers who aspire to the PGA tour commonly start out as assistant pros, giving lessons to members and playing rounds with them while they prove themselves on the various satellite tours that constitute professional golf's minor leagues. Even if they perform well enough to earn their PGA player's card, rookie pros still face a daunting financial challenge. Professional golf is a form of free agency. There are no salaries other than winnings, no expenses paid, no endorsements until you've made a name. And as golf legend Lee Trevino once noted, "You can't putt straight when you're hungry."[9]

Typically at this point, a syndicate, or association, of well-to-do club members funds the early years of the pro's career. Boxers are syndicated the same way. In return for a percentage of earnings, the syndicate will provide a sum of money up front and commit to investing another sum over the term of the arrangement. It's all a crap shoot, very similar to the venture capital funding of new corporations, but at least the members can comfortably assess their asset. As golfers themselves, they benefit psychologically from associating with a potential champ. Now suppose you take your golfer's contract and sell it. You've traded a human-backed security. That's what Maarten LaFeber did. A relatively unknown Dutch player, LaFeber turned his future income stream into a public offering that was oversubscribed tenfold.[10] In effect, he transferred his earnings risk from himself to his investors.

If Tiger Woods had sold equity you could trade, imagine how

much (or little) you could have paid for a share in Woods on or before the first day of the 1997 masters golf tournament. Imagine your profit when Woods won by twelve strokes.

There's no reason for securitization of sports stars to be limited to golf. In January 1999, the Pullman Group announced that it was talking about such securitization with other athletes, starting with basketball, then baseball, and then football.[11]

As with bonds, the next step toward an efficient market for human capital would be to trade such equity. Of course, it will be some time before you can actually trade shares in individuals. The first deals will resemble private placements and venture funding more than IPOs.

Once investors could trade only the securities of big corporations, on the New York Stock Exchange (NYSE). In the early 1900s came the American Stock Exchange (AMEX) and regional exchanges listing smaller companies. In 1971, National Association and Securities Dealers Association Quotations (NASDAQ) offered over-the-counter trading in even smaller corporate entities, including the fledgling Microsoft. Trading in human capital will follow a similar course, as investors take higher risks in these even smaller entities with ever thinner capitalization. And as with bonds, the trend will start with superstars, at the level of a Tiger Woods or a Michael Jordan, then broaden to include a bundle of Internet CEOs, and then finally widen to embrace you.

THE ENABLERS

The logic of future wealth makes this radical innovation in the financial markets an inevitable result of efficient markets for human capital. It raises plenty of how-to questions that we can't yet answer. But we do know that personal securitization will need its own legal, technical, social, and informational infrastructure, just as the factory worker needed all kinds of ancillaries—among them, time clocks, assembly line shifts, child labor laws, paper-pushing foremen, and eventually unions and worker's compensation insurance.

As the opportunities for securitizing intellectual capital multiply, some people will undoubtedly take the money and run, while others will sell themselves into an onerous bondage. Banks that issue mortgage loans face similar risks, and so do issuers of credit cards. They've developed legal and commercial ways to deal with these defaults, and this case will be no different. Maybe we'll see the equivalent of high-interest, high-risk junk bonds for individuals with erratic earning power and behavior.

Securitizing individuals is far from boilerplate work. The practice is still new, and individuals bring individual complications to the table. The Pullman Group, at the forefront of most of these deals to date, has so far engineered only private placements in order to protect its knowledge of how to orchestrate such deals. But the supply (whatever intellectual property or unique skill or talent an individual has that can produce a predictable revenue stream) is eager, and the demand (anyone who invests in tradable securities) is abundant.

To get these willing parties together, the financial services industry will invent countless new wrinkles. Already we've seen the development of the special-purpose vehicle (SPV). A legal entity that exists on paper only, the SPV has a single purpose: to isolate cash flow. The person who signs it transfers to the SPV whatever rights or receipts back a security, and the SPV in turn protects those funds. If one of the Pullman Group's clients were to go bankrupt, for example, the royalties and concert receipts that back that client's bonds or shares wouldn't be gobbled up in the process.

Through such a process, New York City lawyer William Krasilovsky securitized Paul Service's share of the 1980s pop hit "Disco Nights." Service, the drummer with GQ, the group that recorded the song, had been living in the streets. "Disco Nights" produced a steady stream of royalty checks, but never enough to help Service break a cycle of poverty. By securitizing and selling

Service's rights to the song, Krasilovsky created an annuity that pays the ex-drummer $600 a month for seven years,[12] hopefully enough to get him into a stable environment.

Krasilovsky did the same for the Fats Waller estate. Securitizing the rights to "Ain't Misbehavin'," which Waller had sold for $500, helped fund four annual $8,500 scholarships for students of music law at Howard University.[13]

As the demand to trade human capital develops, so will the infrastructure to support it. The same kind of security analysts will be needed to quantify the risk of an individual issuing bonds as are needed for mortgages, equities, and other financial instruments. Personal investment bankers might evolve to help prepare a brand before an individual goes public. Lawyers and bankers will help shape the instruments and put them out to bid. Accountants will have to handle special tax issues. David Pullman, founder, chairman, and CEO of the Pullman Group, predicts that there will be a public market for talent-backed securities within the next five years.[14]

At the other end, the investment community will also be competing for the new business, creating mutual funds with all kinds of specialty interests: the Baker Scholars Fund, Motown's Hit Makers, or, perhaps the most widely constituted fund of all, Kevin Bacon's Co-Stars. The financial innovators who foresee these opportunities will enjoy their own piece of future wealth.

Or imagine this: Take people's publicly available but not widely dispersed credit ratings, and mix them together with other indicators of their station, such as their alma mater, their zip code, the amount of their mortgage, and the kind of car they drive. Develop an algorithm that assigns a composite score as an estimate of financial worth. Then publish everybody's score in the equivalent of a free telephone directory. Now you've reached the HSX stage. Securitizing your family may sound far-fetched, but the prospect of issuing bonds or shares secured by your own talents instead of your home is not. Like it or not, the world is heading in this direction.

Human capital is the world's scarcest resource, and money will follow it, though one never knows its precise path. Once there's a price, there's a future. Once there's a future, there's a trade. Once trading begins, there's a market. The first outcomes will include a more efficient flow of human capital to its highest value use. In addition, a greater share of the return on human capital will be retained by the individuals who own it. This is where you come in.

Future Wealth Expectation: *Tangible assets will start to lose their value as collateral, while intangible human capital becomes bankable.*

6

FROM WORKER TO PLAYER
Securitizing Your Human Capital

TALENT AGENT: *Babe! Babe! You're not hearing me. . . . My guy is not stepping foot in your greenroom until we have a deal . . . including a restructured profit participation on the video and Internet rights! He's tired of performing for peanuts, **especially** on your little cruise ship gigs!*

DEPARTMENT HEAD: *Look, Sid, your boy's not our only option. There's also Schwartz, Taylor, Wycoff . . .*

TALENT AGENT: *Sorry, babe, I rep them, too! This summer I locked up your whole department!*

DEPARTMENT HEAD: *My whole **math** department?*

TALENT AGENT: *You want to talk package? I can go there!*

—GARY TRUDEAU, "Doonesbury"[1]

THE BUSINESS WORLD is finding out how to look at your human assets, your intellectual capital, in a whole new way. You're not going to capitalize your intellectual worth overnight. Meanwhile, the financial industry will be looking at you, developing instruments that will enable investors to value you and trade your abilities and likely future performance. The securitization of human capital is a profound change in our economic structure. It will take considerable time, and we expect the contours of future wealth to form in four ways, each of which will blur into the next.

THE FIRST WAVE: DEMOCRATIZATION OF DEBT

The first of those waves, as we've seen, is already taking place as Bowie Bonds. But securitization, whether traded or not, isn't for everyone at this point. For one thing, only a few of us have the name recognition or personal brand to attract investors to something so novel. Nor, critically, do most of us have the sure and deep cash flow that Bowie's royalties provide. Royalties, after all, continue flowing even after the death of the individual. Just ask Elvis (if he's still in the building).

Over the next couple of years, we'll see more well-known entertainment and sports stars capitalizing their future earnings and turning their multiyear contracts into instant, ready money. As one deal piles onto the next, the financial wrappers and mechanisms will be refined, and the type of packaging will standardize more. Figures of far less renown will start to get into the game as well, perhaps as bundles.

In fact, that blur has already begun. In the music field, both the American Society of Composers, Authors and Publishers (ASCAP) and Broadcast Music Incorporated (BMI), the professional groups that monitor royalties on behalf of composers, arrangers, and performers, have set up mechanisms to connect their members with investors who typically will lend three to four times the member's annual earnings on royalties. Such deals will help bring both the spirit and the mentality of capitalizing future earnings streams down to a level where more people can begin to appreciate it.

THE SECOND WAVE: BROADENING OF THE ASSET BASE

Within five to ten years, we expect a distinct second wave to be under way. This wave will no longer be limited to the superstars of music or sports. Look for highly paid professionals and the best and brightest knowledge workers to get into the act, as investors bundle risk for less well-known personalities. After all, 100 composers with the rights to an average of three songs each have just as many titles collectively, and a similarly predictable, if not equal, income stream, as David Bowie had with 300 of his songs.

As a future asset, it's worth your while to look at how you will be seen through an investor's eye. You can do so by connecting with a number of virtual future wealth exchanges on the Web. We mentioned hsx.com earlier, but you can also check out <www.wall-streetsports.com> to see how David Cone, Greg Maddux, Grant Hill, and Ryan Leaf are traded.

The stock of ever-colorful basketball star Dennis Rodman (RODM) has gone through its own hoops. It dropped sharply from HSX$43 to HSX$39 through the last three weeks of February 1999, amid on-again, off-again rumors that he would join the Los Angeles Lakers. After Rodman put the controversy to rest by signing with the Lakers in late February, his stock picked up considerably, reaching a high of HSX$47 on March 13. On March 14, the Lakers announced that Rodman was taking an indefinite leave of absence, and his stock fell again, to HSX$38 by March 21 and plummeted when the Lakers terminated his contract on April 15. By June 1999, it was trading around HSX$26.[2]

Such fluctuations show how the valuation of human capital changes relative to changes in reputation and performance. These virtual exchanges in human-based securities are wonderful conditioners for the ups and downs that will happen to those of us who do securitize ourselves.

More broadly, we'll see markets grow for the services of scarce human resources. Star surgeons, scientists, and litigators will soon be auctioning their skills and time, as graphic designers and software engineers have already begun to do on Monster.com. As we said before, once there's an auction, there can be futures, and once there are futures, there can be arbitrage. That's when you'll be able to hedge your position in electrical engineers against biotechnician futures, protecting yourself against the earlier-than-expected arrival of the bioeconomy.

THE THIRD WAVE: INSTITUTIONALIZATION OF THE EXCHANGE

Within ten to fifteen years, expect the third wave. We predict that this will take the form of a NASDAQ-like market which deals in people-based financial instruments. Trading rules will have been established, along with formal standards and practices. To bring these exotic securities to market, mutual funds will emerge.

Upstream, on the supply side, bundling will be commonplace. Graduate school classes, all-American basketball teams, McKinsey & Co. alumni associations, X-ray crystallographers, and many more will offer themselves as bundles to be traded publicly and broadly. To make bundling attractive, packagers will reduce each individual's risk by giving a share in the total pool to each member. The rules will resemble microfinancing, but on a macro scale.

Downstream, on the demand side, trading will start thin as it did with Bowie Bonds and grow more interesting. The human bundles will be initially held for long-term investments, but soon juggled in secondary markets like every other security.

In fifteen or so years, those of us who take our intellectual capital to market as a security will see those securities evolve into components of mutual funds that invest in aggregated human capital. Just as surely, investors will want to spread their risk. As a result, your bonds or shares will likely move from one fund to another. Investors will mercilessly dump you at the least provocation, so you can be sure they'll quickly pick up on a bad admissions year for your alma mater.

To win their consistent favor, you'll need a consistent revenue stream, as if you were a business. Individuals will need to adopt the kind of financial reporting standards that companies do and match them with fiscal statements that would meet the approval of the newly minted Individual Financial Accounting Standards Board (IFASB). To that end, you'd need to have the equivalent of an on-line address that would act as your personal 10K or annual report, listing assets and liabilities, and a continually updated résumé. You'd also have to be an active participant in various bulletin boards, offering yourself for jobs and then updating your personal 10K with any new achievements. And all along, of course, you'd be building a network of friends, contacts, associates, competitors, people who offered you jobs in the past, and all the other contacts essential to success.

Self-employment is a precursor of individual capitalization. Until you're a business, you won't have a capital structure. We already know that the next generation will have more jobs than their grandparents. But how much job churn do you have to have before you realize for whom you're really working? Yourself.

"Self-employment" traditionally embraces the likes of farmers, writers, housecleaners, and shopkeepers. "Free agent" is much more than a millennially inspired upgrading of the same idea. It means that you market your services to other entities, previously ones that provided you with the greatest monetary and psychic rewards, but now those that create the greatest appreciation of your human capital, without compromising your freedom to pick and choose.

If individuals take on such a working life, then their distinctive competences in the marketplace—their economic value—derive from themselves, not from their employers. The market knows AOL and Merck, and the quality behind the brands they represent. A free agent without a brand is simply a human commodity, one more coffee bean on the big bush of life. With a brand, you're a distinct, known, and marketable property. Establishing a personal home page might help with your self-branding, but it is barely a start. Expect to see far more extensive efforts as free agents within and throughout the organization work to establish their uniquely marketable assets.

Selling branding and advisory services to individuals is the logical next step. At present, businesses can attract investments more readily than you can as an individual. But that balance will change as human capital becomes a greater source of profits. As that happens, humans will attract capital along lines we now associate with the GEs of the world or Silicon Valley start-ups. New businesses, for example, use investment bankers to do their initial public offerings (IPOs), which offer shares in the company to the public. Just as commercial banking migrated from institutional lending to retail lending more than two decades ago, investment banking will migrate from stars to start-ups—you. Prepare for the retail human capital IPO.

Companies also raise extra money by way of a bond offering, either through an investment bank like Goldman, Sachs or through "commercial paper," which enables them to bypass financial intermediaries and save on the potentially enormous underwriters' fees.

The valuation of intellectual capital will make such financial instruments available to individuals as cornerstones of future wealth. Securitization gives individuals the equivalent of an IPO. It makes them tradable. If individuals are big enough, rich enough, and hip enough—Michael Jordan big, Bill Gates rich, David Bowie hip—then they can issue their own commercial paper. Even those who are none of the above can use their brains rather than their home as a way to securitize their debt. Worried about selling your future? If you make enough, then you can always buy the security back and privatize your fate.

Human giants, of course, will lead this revolution, just as corporate goliaths led the commercial paper chase. But securitization, whatever its ultimate forms, will trickle down to the rest of us in the cascades just described, limited only by the degree to which individuals will accept and adapt to new financial possibilities. Oh, brave new world.

THE FOURTH WAVE: TRADING HUMAN CAPITAL

Twenty years from now, in the fourth wave, some of us will ponder the news that genetic engineers are up two ticks, while animators are off a point and a half. By then, we will probably have an established intellectual capital market, replete with benefits and ills, successes and failures, scandals and shakeouts, as we feel our way. Yes, the players among us will obsess over how the mutual fund that represents us did that day. Indeed, the device that wakes us up twenty years from now will probably tell us our ticker price first thing in the morning: "You're down fifty basis points—you'd better get up now!"

FROM GENERATION TO GENERATION

Who will lead the way? We don't expect the Silent Generation, those born before the baby boomers, to rush to personal securitization—and not just because age tends to breed financial conservatism. The bulk of them retired in the 1980s, flush from the decades-long run-up in the value of both stocks and real estate, and secure in the knowledge that social security would live long enough to do well by them. On the whole, this group is concerned more with preserving the wealth it has than with accumulating more.

Baby boomers, the next generation, will take an interest in securitization, but perhaps not dramatically. For them, future wealth will come largely in the form of what they inherit from their parents—the fruits of the postwar American economic boom that will represent the greatest wealth transfer in human history. As that happens, the attention of boomers will turn away from wealth accumulation to wealth preservation. They'll be interested in securing rather than in risking their assets.

Generation X'ers, those born between 1965 and 1980, face a very different financial future. Rightly suspicious of social security, they believe that they will work well beyond the age at which their parents and grandparents retired. They also want to escape the crushing financial burden of an older generation. As a result, X'ers will likely flock to whatever financial instruments will maximize their return, which means trading risk.

Conditioned by the churn of the workplace, X'ers will also more likely see themselves as individual economic entities, not as players on a corporate team. Intellectually and emotionally, they can more easily leap from "businesses of one" to "financial instruments of one."

Generation Y'ers, those born between 1980 and 1994, appear even more ready to embrace the practices of future wealth. Financial commentator Stephen Pollan cites surveys that show how members of this age group expect to work harder than their predecessors, change jobs and careers more often, and retire far sooner.[3] Their long-range plan is to find their true reward later in life, after they assure their economic security.

Pollan based his findings on a survey of college students, the leading edge of the Gen-Y'ers. He found that 80 percent of them expect to work more than forty-five hours a week at their first job, 64 percent believe they'll change careers at least three times, and an astounding 64 percent also believe they will "retire" before the age of fifty, not to Florida or the golf course, but to jobs, careers, and work that they will find more meaningful and spiritually rewarding than the work that got them there.[4]

Will such people likely securitize their intellectual capital? Will they trade short-term rewards in salary and even stock options for the greater long-term rewards of placing themselves in the financial markets? We think so, and we suspect that the waves of personal securitization will intersect with the rising wave of Gen-Y'ers in both workplace and marketplace.

This scenario underscores that the arrival of future wealth depends not only on innovation in information, financial technology, and regulation, but also on a shift in culture and mind-set. Gen-Y'ers may well yawn at what we find most startling: marketing one's intellectual capital. Given time, and another generation, the financial innovations will overtake even their imaginations. We—and they—would do well to keep in mind these words from Felix Cavaliere, a member of the Young Rascals (a boomer rock group):

And then I'll know that all I've learned, my kid assumes.
And my worst fears are his cartoons.[5]

Future Wealth Expectation: *The day will come when we will put our fifty-two-week trading range on our résumés.*

FROM RISK AS PROBLEM TO RISK AS OPPORTUNITY
Profiting from Uncertainty

I used to worry about getting "outsourced." Today, I'm selling options on my work time 36 months from now.

WE MUST BECOME more and more our own risk managers in all aspects of our lives. To mine future wealth, individuals prepare themselves—intellectually, psychically, and financially—to take risks. Scary as this can be, most of us take more risks than we might think, not only in what we risk, but also in how much of our future wealth we risk. The 401(k)s, IRAs, health care coverage, and all kinds of other benefit plans that we routinely manage involve decisions about risk. Similarly, every time we choose insurance—for our teeth, our car, our house, our poodle, our life—we're making decisions about managing risk.

Risk can be daunting as any four-letter word. Risk puts us at peril. It conjures up the possibility of loss. To calculate the odds, insurance companies employ impenetrable actuarial science: the application of probability and statistics to determine mortality and set rates. Stock pickers use algorithms, coefficients, and standard deviations that to most of us are no more accessible than hiero-glyphics. We know intuitively that reward almost never comes without putting something at risk. But as we'll see in this chapter, future wealth demands that we don't use our attitudes about risking real assets to evaluate risking financial ones.

Historically, with our tangible real assets comes the risk of tangi-ble loss, and with that, risk-averse behavior. For example, to lay off, or sell, the risk of losing our property to mishaps or thieves, we buy insurance—for our crops, home, car, boat, jewelry, anything that we value highly. The risk of physically losing the tangible asset isn't diminished in either case, but buying insurance protects us against the loss of the wealth the asset represents. We happily pay the pre-mium that represents the average risk with 100 percent certainty, rather than play the odds and most likely get off scot-free. Of course, the chance that our house will burn down is pretty remote, and almost all of us would end our lives richer if we forgot about buying insurance and bore the risk ourselves. The insurance company, of course, gladly does business with us. It pools our individual risk with those of thousands of others, sure that the odds are on its side.

Let's face it; most of us were brought up to be careful. Risk aver-sion went with good manners and thrift—and with holding down a well-paid, secure job. But remember, *saving* is just the word we use to convince ourselves that our investments are safe. Once, "safe investments" meant the mattress, and then the circa-1900 bank account. After the big surprise of the depression, a federally insured, low-interest bank account or a savings bond, also backed by the government, became the way to save. Now, as people gain more control over their wealth and have more of it, risk *aversion* is dangerous, causing us to leave more money on the table than we can afford. We need to see the opportunity side of risk, as well as the threat. At first, incorporating this perspective into our behavior seems totally foreign. It certainly requires a major attitude adjustment, but in fact many of us, willingly or not, are already treating risk as opportunity.

We make dozens of risk decisions and calculations every day, with regard to every element of our wealth. Run a yellow light, and you're making a risk-reward choice: At risk are your real assets (your car) and your human assets (your health), and if you're sued, your financial assets, too. On the other hand, running the light perhaps paid you the reward of time saved. The decision isn't consciously made—we'd be paralyzed if we thought through every such choice—but risk and reward are at stake all the same. Different risks and rewards are at stake, too, when your sixteen-year-old son asks for the car on a Saturday night, or your college-age daughter announces that she wants to spend the summer backpacking solo across Europe. Yet our children have to learn responsibility sometime, and nearly all of them are going to leave home eventually.

Risk and reward choices are unavoidable, whether we think of them in those terms or not. For most of us, too, they've become an unavoidably larger part of our lives. A half-generation back, most employee health benefit plans offered a bare minimum by way of choice: an HMO-approved doctor, perhaps, versus the right to choose your own doctor at a higher monthly premium. Today, many workers face a cafeteria of choices, each of which requires them to weigh risk against reward. Take a higher deductible to reduce overall cost, and you're betting that you'll have a healthy year. Opt out of the expensive dental plan, and the potential reward of more cash on hand is offset by the potential risk of having to pay for crowns and repairing broken molars. The HMO, in turn, is trading its own risks with your risks. If you choose the full-coverage, low-deductible plan and are struck with a catastrophic illness, you win as measured by financial capital, even if you lose in terms of your human capital.

Notice how financial risk is creeping into our daily lives. In the examples above, some risks are between real alternatives (does the son who borrows your car end up injured or coddled?). Some trade real risks against financial ones (if your house burns down, you get the money to buy another one). Some are purely financial (investing in a stock instead of a bond).

Financial risk ascends. Decisions about pay have already pushed us in this direction. They're nowhere so straightforward as they once were. Agree to postpone a raise in favor of stock options, and assume the risk that the company will go bust or that its stock price will never climb high enough to yield much by way of profit. Some companies will offer you a choice between fixed compensation and putting some at risk to gain an upside.

In fact, planning for retirement—all those 401(k) plans, IRAs, Keoghs, and the like—provides an endless lesson in risk-reward management. How much of those funds do we put at minimal risk, how much at maximum risk? How do the tax protections of retirement plans affect those calculations? And how have we protected ourselves against the risk of inflation? Of currency fluctuation? Can we trust social security to carry us through? If a portion of our social security funds is opened up to private investment, even this most paternalistic of government programs will no longer be quite so fatherly. If this comes to pass, then risk management will have worked its way still further into the daily lives of the citizenry.

All of us trade risks all the time. Most of us, however, don't necessarily know that we do. We like to think that we choose among options whose outcomes are pretty certain when they're really not. The earth quakes, the market tanks, and the Fortune 500 company topples.

These catastrophes actually happen with surprising frequency. Research shows that people underestimate the likelihood of radical change by a factor of ten or so. In other words, what you think happens only one time in a hundred actually occurs one time in ten—that's what makes them surprises! In our desire for certainty, we ignore the data and delude ourselves that risk is not an important part of our lives. In the real economy, this attitude serves us by lowering our anxieties about what we can't control. In the world of future wealth, ignoring risk means kicking opportunity in the teeth.

MANAGING YOUR RISK PORTFOLIO

Consciously or not, most of us are affected by three factors when we make a decision about risk. First, there's the basic math in a risk. In roulette, for example, the house wins most of the time because there are thirty-eight slots in the wheel but hitting your number only pays thirty-six to one. Second is the completeness of information about the situation. Know the hurricane patterns before you buy or insure a beach house. And third is your personal risk profile. Some of us keep our money in a savings account because we can't bear the downside of the stock market. Others are so enamored of risk that they end up dying on Mount Everest.

Managing risk means dealing with all three. Our beach house owner might forgo storm insurance and invest his money in the stock market instead, on the risk-accepting theory that the market will yield more than any damage would cost. Conversely, a risk-averse college quarterback facing a bright career in the NFL might insure his throwing arm against disabling injury on the theory that, because his future earning power depends on one appendage, he must insure it. Whether we're risk accepting or risk averse, the potential loss of wealth inherent in a real tangible asset is a problem, so we tend to surrender a little or a lot through insurance premiums to protect against it.

In contrast, to avoid the erosion of our financial assets, we invest them. We might buy shares or real estate that we think will climb in value far faster than mutual funds. By doing so, we increase our risk exposure to stay ahead of inflation and increase our purchasing power. Here, too, the degree to which we take on risk depends on our individual risk preferences. Those who like risk can put their assets into high-yield, high-risk junk bonds or options, or even rare art, while those who don't can keep their cash in a money market account or hunker into low-paying bonds backed by the full faith and credit of the U.S. government.

Remember, you limit downside financial risk through *insurance*, paying a fee that is certain, and you limit upside risk through conservative *investments*, earning a return that is all but certain. You should also remember that the more you limit upside risk, the more you limit opportunity.

During much of history, of course, wealth and the risk decisions that came with it weren't an issue for most people. Whatever meager wealth passed from generation to generation typically accumulated in the form of real assets, such as the family farm, store, or silver. The instinct and the approach to wealth creation were slow accumulation and protection, and risk was a problem that most were happy to trade away if the opportunity arose—rent your land to a peasant and you needn't worry about crop failure.

The truly wealthy, those with significant real *and* financial assets, have long had a different approach to risk. When F. Scott Fitzgerald wrote in *The Great Gatsby* that "the rich are different from you and me," he had in mind all sorts of social differences, but one of them could well have been a different behavior with respect to risk. Sure, the rich have more money. But instead of insuring against the loss of their wealth, they typically seek to increase it through trading risk and through the opportunities that come along with it.

Of course, one reason that the rich may be more inclined to take risks is that they can afford to lose. If you have a dozen houses around the world, perhaps you're best served by being your own insurance company.

As it was with the rich in Fitzgerald's day, so it is with many more of us now. Across the whole spectrum of the middle class, wealth in terms of accumulated stuff is losing importance relative to financial wealth. The latest data available from the Federal Reserve's Survey of Consumer Finances, for instance, show that the ratio of financial to nonfinancial assets held by U.S. households increased by half in just six years (from 34 percent in 1989 to 51 percent in 1995).[1] Before long, money, more than silver or real estate, is what will be handed down from one generation to the next, not just for the Gatsbys but for the nation.

What does all this have to do with managing risk? When wealth meant illiquid assets, insurance was our primary risk management tool. As liquid assets assume parity for many of us, we find ourselves in an interesting place. We're still not Gatsby rich. We can't invest millions of our own, for example, in some high-flying private placement. But we can't afford to ignore the upside opportunity by locking all our money in savings accounts. We need to consider everything from Asian mutual funds to Internet start-ups.

If you're born rich, then you know how to take risks and live with them. If you're very new to all this, you're going to need help, just as the very rich surround themselves with advisers. Otherwise, you'll be awake all night, imagining spending your retirement on a park bench.

THE CONNECTED ECONOMY TO THE RESCUE

The connected economy has introduced millions of individuals to a Wall Street that once was open to only a select clientele. In pursuit of the fulfillment of their desires, ordinary individuals now can trade not only stocks and bonds, but also derivatives and other kinds of sophisticated financial instruments.

What's more, the various asset management plans offered by most brokerage houses allow investors to move fluidly between high-risk stocks, safer indexed mutual funds, money market accounts, and anywhere else they wish to trade their wealth under the brokerage house's umbrella.

Increasingly, they can do so through an electronic marketplace. E-trading has made portfolios part of our daily lives and forever changed the way we think about money, investing, and wealth. In 1996, the technology hardly registered on the national consciousness. One year later, 7 percent of all equity trades were executed electronically. In 1998, the number doubled, to 14 percent. By 1999, the number of on-line accounts had grown to more than 7 million, and day traders alone accounted for about 10 percent of NASDAQ's trading volume.

Most of these transactions aren't being made by investors who took their business away from the established full-service broker-ages. No doubt, soaring markets lured many new investors. But their entry was eased by the dramatically lower cost of getting infor-mation and of completing a transaction. Buying $10,000 worth of stocks costs between $10 and $30 in commissions at an electronic broker, compared to more than $100 at a full-service broker, with discount brokers falling somewhere in between. And the trade is something you can do in your PJs, while brushing your teeth before going to bed, or first thing in the morning between watching CNN and leaving for work. Pretty soon they'll put a Bloomberg terminal in McDonalds so you can trade over your Egg McMuffin.

A large part of the savings on these and other deals over the Net is possible because intermediaries—brokers, dealers, agents—are increasingly dropping from the equation. And why not? When the principals in a deal can trade directly with one another across cyberspace, who needs intermediaries?

Maybe you do. In return for the minimal charge of e-trading, individuals are getting minimal advice. They become not only their own brokers but also their own investment advisers. The evidence is beginning to suggest that, as they do so, they become both more comfortable with risk—and more inclined to pursue higher rewards.

A 1999 study by the research firm NFO Worldwide compared the portfolios of Internet users who invest on-line with those of people who don't. It found that the latter kept 52 percent of their financial assets in mutual funds, 28 percent in other securities, and only 20 percent in individual stocks. On-line investors, in contrast, had 43 percent of their financial assets in mutual funds, 10 percent in other securities, and 47 percent in stocks—nearly two-and-a-half times the percentage of individual stocks.[2] But this comfort with risk has not been tested recently by a difficult market. Comfort doesn't confer competence.

The elimination of intermediaries, assuming they know their business, increases the risk that the unsophisticated can lose more on the stock market than they can afford. The long bull run has convinced many professional investors that they can do no wrong, so why should amateurs be any less gullible?

The connected economy is doing exactly what anybody who's been paying attention would predict. It is democratizing markets for risk, creating all kinds of financial packages that can be traded in small quantities. As the markets start trading in human capital, these new instruments, too, will be available to individual investors. It's your opportunity—and responsibility—to be ready for this. Are you?

LIVING WITH RISK

Persuading individuals to take any risks at all, particularly with their retirement funds, was initially a tough sell, sometimes because of their inborn resistance to change, sometimes because of an aversion to making their own decisions. The big surprise is how quickly most of us in the United States have become accustomed to being masters of our own future financial well-being.

Baby boomers and their children are coming to believe that their future wealth, particularly the money they'll have at retirement, depends more heavily on their skills as pickers of mutual funds than it does on their current income, social security, or defined pensions that will be paid by their employers. Many Americans in their sixties and seventies are already talking about the size of their portfolio rather than the size of their pension.

Such a portfolio would certainly include the usual elements of financial capital: stocks, bonds, mutual funds, and derivatives, many of them purchased electronically. Financial assets, remember, are built for speed because they are generally both liquid and fungible.

How about real capital—cars, art, our homes? Most people still see these tangible goods as real capital—that is, as illiquid. Such a viewpoint leads them to retain a risk-averse attitude to insure themselves against loss. That makes sense. But two things will happen.

First, more of us will lease a car rather than buy one, to preserve more of our wealth as financial, and thus easily investable, capital. In other words, our greater tolerance for risk will lead us to leverage our real assets by turning them into cash. The cash we raise with a second mortgage can be placed at risk in stocks or mutual funds. Just think, the welcome mat at the front door may soon say, "Home, Sweet Financial Opportunity!"

More importantly, eBay and others to come are in fact liquefying our real assets. Never use the home gym equipment? Your kids too rambunctious for that antique? Once, you could unload such things only at a yard sale, and even then you'd get only pennies. Electronic auctions are creating profitable second markets for just about everything. Your possessions are almost as liquid as the shares you have in your financial portfolio. Now you can bring a risk management attitude to every*thing* that you buy and own.

So far, we haven't touched on what we claimed in the last chapter was the most valuable asset in the connected economy, the one traded on the least liquid of markets. The securitization of human capital will make human assets every bit as liquid as the rest of an investment portfolio. Our portfolios will contain real, financial, and human asset investments.

The most exciting security of all, of course, is our own human capital. (But enough about future wealth. What about *my* future wealth?) Your most important asset is the one you were born with and have invested in all your life, with the possible exception of the 1960s, if you're a boomer. The most important investment decision you make is what you do with it. How you invest it and how much risk you take with it affect every other element in your portfolio.

For a few, this scenario is already familiar. An actress works as a waitress, glad to take the risk of finally landing that part. A trust fund heir works pro bono to groom himself for a risky run for elective office. Both forgo financial return to invest in their human capital, which may appreciate substantially in the future.

For most of us, such risk trade-offs are a new and scary concept. If you thought it was tough selecting a mutual fund for your 401(k), you ain't seen nothin' yet. You'll be choosing how and when to securitize yourself, paying a lot more attention to your own market cap than to someone else's IPO.

At the same time, you'll want to manage the risk of personal flame-out by buying hedges against the particular risks that confront you. You can attempt to do this by yourself, trading illiquid assets on eBay, liquid assets on eTrade, and human assets on Monster.com, HSX, or some future eBrain. Just as financial reports and analysts support your financial trading, new reporting standards and information sources for human and real risks will arise.

The financial industry is sure to be all over these new developments, pushing all kinds of advice and capabilities. Someone will come up with a risk management account, analogous to Merrill Lynch's cash management account which revolutionized retail finance in the 1980s. It will be designed to help you manage all your upside and downside risks as an integrated portfolio. First, the super wealthy will opt for the private risk manager who leads a team comprised of a financial engineer, agent, psychological counselor, and auctioneer. Then it will seep down into the just wealthy and next into the middle classes. Eat your heart out, Jay Gatsby!

Future Wealth Expectation: *Households will come to see themselves as risk managers, and financial institutions will create Risk Rationalization Accounts to help them.*

PART III

companies

INDIVIDUALS ARE LEADING the way, but future wealth also belongs to those companies that recognize the racing tide and ride it, like a surfer on a wave. To avoid being swamped, companies must start thinking differently. They must come to see themselves as offering the best return on their workers' human capital; when the fit isn't there, they'll encourage their workers to move on but they might buy a piece of their future.

This isn't the time for swimming against the tide. Companies need to wade into the future themselves, as full participants. They must clock themselves in real time, and measure and value themselves constantly by future performance, not past. Annual reports, for example, are autopsies, showing only where a company has been. Companies need to do for themselves just what the financial markets do to them.

Risk managers are an integral part of how a company will do business in the world of future wealth. Managing risk is as important as what we do or make. And as we said about individuals, a company that won't take risks is taking the biggest risk of all.

8

FROM SBUs TO SRUs
Managing Strategic Risk

For the first time in years, CEO Jeff Greene slept like a baby. Gone were the nightmares of sneering analysts, furious shareholders, and tumbling share prices. His operating earnings would meet predictions, no matter what. Bankrupt customers, vanishing suppliers, and all the other risks over which he had no control had been taken care of, guaranteed by an insurance company that would make up any shortfall in his pretax results. With dreams of a jubilant second quarter swirling in his head, Greene murmured contentedly and turned over, happy with an insurance premium well spent.

THOUGH WE CAN'T VOUCH for CEO sleep patterns, we can say that such insurance policies do exist—evidence that efficient markets will develop to trade everything, including every kind of downside risk.

Reliance Insurance Company has already introduced policies that it can tailor to cover almost any risk to a company's operating results.[1]

Insurance is the traditional way to manage risk, an intrinsic part of future wealth. Every company must build not only a system that allows it to measure and manage all that it does by the risks involved, but also a culture that informs and supports risk-taking behavior in its talent.

Many may choose to offer someone else this risk/reward to manage and mine. Before they do, companies should consider setting up what we'll call "strategic risk units" (SRUs) within the corporation. These SRUs would enable a corporation to isolate and clearly identify risks. Then they could manage them directly or trade them in the financial markets, perhaps by selling them to insurance companies, perhaps by hedging themselves.

ISOLATING RISK

In one sense, SRUs mirror the strategic business units, or SBUs, now at many companies. Whereas SBUs focus on a specific set of products or services and their markets, SRUs would identify, evaluate, differentiate, package, and trade the various risks a company faces. Many capital-intensive firms and financial intermediaries already practice some form of risk management. Some—primarily financial firms like Fidelity Investments or Bankers' Trust—have chief risk officers to keep track of the portfolio of risks their companies are bearing. An SRU would go further, perhaps consolidating a company's other risks that *cross* SBUs or separating low-risk from high-risk enterprises to unleash constrained revenue potential, such as eSchwab.com from Charles Schwab & Co.; DLJ*direct* from its parent Donaldson, Lufkin & Jenrette; or bn.com from Barnes & Noble.

Rain could help Disney's box office receipts, for example, but harm theme park attendance. Should Disney have weather hedges, an insurance policy that will pay up when the rain falls down? An

SRU would look across all weather-related risks, in all countries where Disney operates, and examine its exposure. Then it might be able to offer this risk package to a group specializing in such instruments, or choose to keep the risk itself. There might be an SRU for weather and for each of the major risks facing the business.

Even more in tune with the theme of future wealth, SRUs would be a "pure play" in risk. Investors are fond of taking on a specific kind of risk, not a complex compound of many. Investors like diversified portfolios of risks, but they like to control the proportions themselves, not have the ingredients made into a stew according to each company's recipe. For example, they've favored Texas Instruments more as TI has shed some of its nonchip businesses, giving investors a purer play in microchips. SRUs would create pure plays for downside risks, packaged for the financial markets and traded by those who understand or want to trade a particular risk—agricultural futures for agronomists, for example, or monsoons for meteorologists.

SBUs already manage risk, in that they monitor a company's exposure to such real-sector factors as: Will the price be too high or too low? Will the order be too early or too late? Will the supplier meet our deadlines? Will we have enough capacity? Will the customer like our product? Still, if the real sector had no risks, then there would be no rewards.

SBUs and SRUs would complement one another because they come at risk for entirely different purposes. SBUs minimize real risk and see financial vistas as ancillary. SRUs would look for financial risk, the better to leverage and trade it. You might say that GMAC started as an SRU with General Motors, and now its profits are earned as an SBU, and growing faster than the auto SBU.

PURSUING RISK

A company that installs SRUs may have pulled the plug on "playing it safe," a long-lived corporate dogma. Traditionally, a smart manager has known how to minimize risk through control procedures. Market testing, management supervision, insurance, learning from other people's mistakes, and the budgeting process were all sound approaches. Budget "sandbagging," common at many companies, took risk avoidance to the pathological level: Managers set a business' goals so low that they'd never miss their targets. As a result, the company was guaranteed never to reach its full potential. The flip side, setting overly aggressive goals, meant taking on too much risk, including that of a manager's failure. In short, most corporate cultures made it clear that the priority for any given project was not to overachieve or underachieve, but to come in "on plan." In other words, "no surprises." After all, Wall Street punishes surprises.

Companies justify such behavior by claiming that shareholders have a short-term focus on quarterly results. The proper goal, therefore, is to make quarterly earnings—to be predictable at the expense of pursuing aggressive goals.

Internet companies escape this Wall Street pressure. In fact, they appear to bask in a diametrically opposite set of standards. Their stocks reach astronomical market capitalizations even though the companies themselves may never have made a profit. More astounding yet, these companies won't tell Wall Street, or anybody else, just when they might move into the black. Super investor Warren Buffet avoids such stocks precisely because he doesn't know what they are worth. Buffett once suggested a way for business schools to teach the principles of valuing companies. "I would say for a final exam: Here's the stock of any Internet company; what's it worth? And anybody who gave an answer flunked."[2]

We aren't arguing with America's second richest man. Our point is not that Internet companies are over- or undervalued. Investments in many dot.com companies may prove foolish, but the trend toward long-term growth and profitability of this sector is not. The point is that companies that set aggressive goals for themselves create investment opportunities for an underserved market looking for measurable risk. Far from being a threat to value, risk today creates value, especially for companies that learn to package their risks in ways the market can understand, price, and trade. Many investors prefer a clear picture of their exposure, the pure play once again, to a company of overly entangled risks. SRUs would separate, organize, and clarify them. Who knows? Perhaps someone beyond the producer of *Baywatch* will find a career in exposure marketing.

PACKAGING RISK

Appropriately, the insurance industry leads in separating, defining, clarifying, and trading risks. Consider the following example, disguised at the insurer's request. During the Malaysian currency crisis, the country attempted to finance a power project but found the cost prohibitive because of the poor rating given to the proposed bond issue, which would be backed by the project's sale of power. Investors perceived both a revenue risk (Malaysia might not recover soon enough to need the power) and a currency risk (the ringgit might fall further).

Enter the insurance companies. They pointed out that separating these risks would make the bonds more attractive. They offered a guarantee of the level of revenues, isolating the currency risk. Since the world financial markets understand the trading of currency risks better than they do the Malaysian power market, the project was able to market this risk effectively, at a better bond rating. This use of "insurance capital" saved the project more in reduced interest cost than it absorbed in insurance premium.

Other companies are creatively laying off risks, too. In 1998, British Aerospace insured the revenues of a leasing subsidiary. Backed by nine insurance companies, the policy insured the company for generating $3.7 billion in revenues over the next fifteen years. If not, the insurers will help fill the shortfall. To the company, the improved level and certainty of aircraft sales offset the cost of the insurance. In airlines again, GE has been bearing the risk formerly assumed by airlines by charging for jet engines per hour of use, rather than selling them outright. If the engine fails, it's GE's problem, not their customers', and GE is in the best position to assess the risk over its whole population of engines. Along the way, GE gets to observe the behavior of its entire fleet, helping it build more reliable engines in the future. Times Mirror Co., publisher of the Los Angeles *Times* and other newspapers and magazines, bought a policy that protects the company from increases in the price of newsprint, the largest industry cost, which is subject to volatile price swings.[3] If the price of paper exceeds specified levels, then the insurer will cover some of the difference.

SHARING RISK

How do shareholders fare in such deals? As we've said, limiting upside risk also limits the opportunity for greater reward. At British Aerospace's leasing company, the amount of the premiums reduces earnings. On the other hand, the company can better predict its revenue stream and increase its growth prospects. At Times Mirror, protection against newsprint price swings also hits earnings, but it removes volatility from the share price. Investors can bet on the newspaper business that they understand as a pure service play rather than the commodity-price-driven paper makers. And shareholders at any insurance company can rejoice over additional premiums.

Are earnings insurance policies—or even insurance policies for earnings-per-share and share-price movements—the things of the future? Not too long ago we would have answered with an unequivocal "No." But in January 1999, Reliance Insurance offered a policy that insures corporate earnings against punitive swings in oil prices and other surprises. Such policies understandably exclude shortfalls caused by strikes or changes in accounting practices. The Reliance policy differs from the Malaysian situation. Rather than untangle risks to sell each separately to the highest bidder, it binds various risks together and transfers them to their shareholders, who are in the business of managing such risks.[4]

Insurance companies, of course, primarily separate and bear financial risk. By their very nature, their lines of business are centered on SRUs. To them, the customer's dread of theft, fire, flood, and earthquake are hand-rubbing opportunities. The industry is moving into its future wealth by further slicing, dicing, and re-pooling the market to create more opportunities. But as the Times Mirror example shows, noninsurance companies can also create future wealth for themselves by pursuing the same kinds of risk-trading opportunities that insurers create. That would be part of any effective SRU manager's job description.

The same separation of risk is pushing U.S. companies to separate their high-growth divisions for packaging to the financial markets as "tracking stocks." These equity issues give investors a pure play in a subsidiary. Such stocks provide a way for companies to unleash the value of their best divisions without spinning them off, selling them, or creating separate corporate entities. *Business Week* reported that there were thirty-six tracking stocks on the market as of June 1999. Ziff-Davis, for example, issued tracking stock in its on-line ZDNet subsidiary, and Donaldson, Lufkin & Jenrette similarly issued stock in its DLJ*direct* Internet unit.[5] You might think that such stocks wouldn't work because they have no separate claims on the parent company's assets. But investors love them, bidding up the value of companies after this virtual disaggregation. Not surprisingly, more tracking stocks are in the pipeline from companies ranging from DuPont to Microsoft.

ORGANIZING AROUND RISK

In essence, we are suggesting that the chief risk officer and the SRU general manager are inseparable—that running an SBU without a risk perspective is not doing the whole job. Companies could implement SRUs as part of their organizations' structure to replace

SBUs, but persuading the members of an SBU to identify and strategically manage their risk will be an uphill battle, and involve a lot of relearning. After all, the SBU habitually thinks in terms of the real sector, and the SRU thinks in terms of the financial sector: create, manage, organize, and trade risk. The CFO is likely to see the introduction of risk considerations by SRU managers as outright interference. To mollify him, a company could charge SBUs a transfer price for risk, adjusting their cost of capital to their specific risks, and then manage aggregated risks at the corporate level, as it would with foreign currency. We could imagine companies organizing separate units around each risk, though these would come to resemble financial companies and might effectively get spun.

Even though publicly traded companies understand that they serve the financial sector through share prices, most doubt that they serve a larger financial market, a marketplace for risk. They pay for such myopia. *A company that sees itself operating purely in the real sector blinds itself to the lucrative risk-trading by-products of its core business.*

TRADING RISK

That said, a few companies *are* getting the message. And although their industries vary widely, they share a common concern: the weather. In fact, the weather derivatives market is a hot one and has surged to about 100 deals a month, according to Jack Cogen, president of NatSource, an over-the-counter broker of energy products and financial products derived from weather and the environment.[6] Examples include a coat manufacturer that insured itself against winters that were too warm and a seller of swimming pools that was worried about water shortages.

Rain falls on a company's customers and suppliers, creating more opportunities to trade risk. Bombardier, a Canadian aerospace and snowmobile company, offered a $1,000 rebate to buyers of its Ski-Doo machines in sixteen U.S. cities if the local snowfall was less than half the average of that in the past three years. Bombardier itself assumed the risk that its customers traditionally carried when buying machines in a snow-free season. Bombardier in turn hedged its bet with snowfall options. The company paid Enron Corp. between $45 and $400 for each snowmobile sold, and Enron agreed to reimburse Bombardier the full $1,000 for every rebate paid. Ski-Doo sales in the sixteen cities soared 38 percent over the year before.[7]

Ancor Communications, a switch manufacturer in Minnetonka, Minnesota, had revenues of less than $10 million in 1998 and was losing more than that. Ancor has a promising technology that could produce real shareholder value, but only if a high-tech customer would buy from a young company with no track record. Ancor approached computer manufacturer Sun Microsystems with 1.5 million unvested warrants (options to buy shares) as a sales premium. When fully vested, the warrants represented 4.5 percent of Ancor's equity. The warrants would vest only in proportion to what Sun bought from Ancor. To vest all warrants, Sun would have to buy $100 million worth of Ancor switches by 2002, certainly a big deal for a small firm. The more Sun buys, the more it gets of Ancor's equity, a prize that doubles as a discount on its purchases—and a capital gain. Ancor's share price more than tripled over the next few weeks. The more switches Sun buys, the less risky its stake in Ancor becomes.[8]

The Medicines Company, or TMC, a pharmaceutical development firm in Cambridge, Massachusetts, has become a skilled buyer and seller of risk as an offshoot of its core business. Developing a drug can cost about $300 million and entails five distinct stages, from developing the chemical or biological compound to winning approval from the Food and Drug Administration (FDA). The potential upside, of course, is another billion-dollar blockbuster like Tagamet, Zantac, or Viagra.

TMC understood that drug development represents a sequence

of very different risks, because a drug can fail for different reasons at any point in the approval process. The later the failure, the more expensive the failure. TMC had a clear sense of the risks it managed well, particularly the risk of failure during clinical trials. It was weak upstream in basic research and downstream in marketing drugs to physicians. So the company concentrates on buying the rights to chemical and biological compounds, developing them into drugs and then selling them to other pharmaceutical firms to bring to market. As a result, TMC has developed a successful business of buying and selling drug development projects. The company bears risk only for the pieces of the process where it best knows how to succeed.

RISK MANAGEMENT AS A CORE COMPETENCY

If "core competencies" help a company focus on value creation in the real sector, then the SRU concept will help it profit from its risk exposures. A company will know which risks to take (as Sun did) and which to lay off (as Times Mirror did). Many muddled business strategies will become much clearer once a company can show that it knows how to price, bear, and trade risk.

Companies are already considering risk as an organizing principle. Banks and other financial companies invest vast sums in risk management systems, as a way to protect themselves against currency swings and the like. Like many other financial institutions, Chase Manhattan Bank has formalized this activity and has a vice chairman for finance and risk management. Real options approaches help acknowledge that surprises create and destroy more value than certainty and that they appear more often than we expect. Our future wealth expectations have more to do with our risks than with our assured cash flows.

The chief risk officer has come to all kinds of companies. Typically, the CRO manages and trades a corporation's business and financial risks and educates employees on managing risk. Some

CROs will choose to outsource at least some of their risk, trading it to insurers eager to bear and manage it. Other CROs will do everything in-house.

The real and financial risks come together in the use of "real options," a relatively new development of the finance world. Historically, most companies have looked at major investments as all-or-nothing commitments, when in fact there are often many other options—walk away in the middle, sell the rights to develop the drug to someone else at an early stage. Real options provide real-sector managers with a risk management perspective on their major business decisions. Risk management itself affords them the chance to adjust their exposure.

For the past twenty years, companies have been struggling to focus on the customers who bought their products or services, and SBUs were one mechanism for doing this. To build future wealth, companies must come to see that customers for their risks are every bit as important. Without them, a company won't be able to attract the new kinds of investors who want to put their money, not into the stock of an SBU, but into a pure-play risk. And every business manager will need explicitly to be a risk manager. What a company does with its risks is an integral part of its future wealth.

Future Wealth Expectation: *Risk will become an explicit dimension of management reporting.*

FROM INSIDE TO OUTSIDE
Running Your Organization by Marketplace Rules

Freedom has many difficulties and democracy is not perfect, but we have never had to put up a wall to keep our people in, to prevent them from leaving us.

—JOHN F. KENNEDY, Berlin, 1963

COMPANIES PUT UP WALLS of all kinds, all the time. And by doing so, they restrict the movement of their people, the flow of information between them and the market, and ultimately all opportunities. Only by evolving at the speed of the connected economy, and not navel gazing, can a company stay in business.

If you hand control to the marketplace, then you'll be amazed at how quickly changes will be made. The organizer that your company needs most is the market.

External change takes place exponentially, internal change takes place arithmetically. When a change happens outside, it triggers repeated cascades of economic changes among customers, suppliers, and competitors, each altering the others. When a change is made inside, the ripple effect is lessened by power struggles, politics, culture, status, and organizational inertia. The filters imposed by organizations are so strong that, even if external economics work their way in, it's too late. A gap has opened between where your organization is and where your business needs to be. What's more, the faster things change out there, the greater and more dangerous is the gap between your company's internal and external worlds.

Into this gap pour all those who help organizations change. The more deeply you buy into whatever organizational theory your guru favors, the more thoroughly trapped you are likely to be. Say you adopt the hot organizational principle of the year 2000 and take the minimum two years to change hearts, minds, and systems. When you're done, in 2002, you'll have an organization perfectly suited for . . . 2000.

So forget about designing organization. Internal transfer prices, for example, are as inadequate within for-profit corporations as they are between government-run and -owned companies in regulated economies, and in those with central planning. Operate your business by the rules of the market, and you'll enjoy the same advantages that propelled market economies ahead of the planned economies of the world. Hewlett-Packard, for example, has created a two-way auction market for securities whose value depends on how many computers the company sells during a particular future period. The bid that matches actual sales pays a dividend, and in nineteen test runs, the market mechanism proved a better predictor than in-house forecasts.

The bottom line? Because the external pace of change is greater than the internal pace, the only solution is to make sure that your internal organization runs by marketplace rules.

OPEN YOUR BORDERS . . .

Despite their competitive analyses, bidding processes, and industry associations, companies suffocate themselves with centrally planned budgets, network fire walls, and packaged communications to employees.

Meanwhile, as you must know by now, electronic connections are bringing efficient markets to every part of the economy. Yet the same design engineer who uses a software agent to compare on-line prices of the latest Kurt Cobain memorial CD gets told by the purchasing department to pay only so much for grommets—or to buy them from a particular supplier.

The Internet and all other electronic connections with outsiders reduce the costs of quickly finding, buying, and getting what you need from people outside the organization. Friction-free capitalism makes internal organization obsolete. The market rules outside, power rules inside.

Ironically, as Peter Drucker points out, "Computers have done a great deal of harm by making managers even more inwardly focused. Executives are so enchanted by the internal data the computer generates—and that's all it generates so far, by and large—they have neither the mind nor the time for the outside. Yet results are only on the outside."[1]

Many tried to expand their vision by building "extranets"—separate information systems carefully kept apart from the intranets already in place. They saw only downside risk to blurring the internal fixtures of administrative power with the chaos of efficient markets. Their hearts were in the right place, but not their networks.

Inter matters more than intra. Intranets are designed to link internal employees with one another and to grow organization. Extranets link people across organizations and grow business. The Internet resolves the conflict, linking the smallest and largest players, and erasing the boundary between inside and outside. By burrowing through internal silos and the corporate perimeter, the Internet blurs the internal and external, the business and organization. Doing business within your firm may even be riskier than doing business with the outside world. Let's face it: Without a culture of risk, an employee won't connect with the guy in the next cube, let alone the customer across the world!

. . . AND LET THE MARKET IN

The fact is, what's happening in the outside world permeates every company. Connectivity attaches everyone to the marketplace. The result is that the "factors of production" that companies use to make their stuff—raw materials, plant and equipment, and labor— are increasingly obtained "just in time" in the marketplace, rather than owned "just in case." Remember, Ford once had iron mines and steel factories and, through long-term union contracts, essentially owned its labor force, too. Today, GE auctions off its demand for materials and supplies, and Cyrix makes chips in random silicon foundries. Self-employment, as we have noted, is growing faster than any other kind. Support services are bought from outside. Outsourcing legal services is nothing new, but having Kinko's come into your office to set up and operate your mailroom is.

Now you have no idea who the guys at the watercooler really work for. Whoever they are, your company is more efficient because, when you deal with outsiders, you are operating by marketplace laws of supply and demand, which is not the case when your transactions are internal. Internally, costs are blurred, fudged, and buried as overhead. Contract out a part, service, or function, and competitive market forces will allow you to gauge such factors as price, time, and quality.

This is not about outsourcing as a way to get lean and still keep the walls up. Even if you have no intention of buying outside, you should still look beyond your own borders. You're obliged to look out in the marketplace for a reality check.

Each element of the organization must be competing in an external marketplace, not just supplying internal customers. Your mailroom? Its performance should be better than Kinko's, or you shouldn't be running it. Product engineering? Why not outsource to IDEO and other design-for-hire companies? Information systems? Don't even think of custom coding—buy a software package and hire a systems integrator. Factory production? Consider outsourcing from custom manufacturing facilities. Why would any company think that it can run a peripheral cost center better than an outside firm can run that same activity as a full-time business?

Then, make sure that the competencies you keep in-house are competing in the market for what they do. Think of them as separate companies. Here's a practical challenge: Make sure every internal group sells more than 20 to 40 percent of its services in the open market. This means that the internal price will have to be in real currency, not the funny money called "internal transfer price."

If your people can't sell their services outside, then either the market doesn't want your people's services (in which case, why do you?), or someone outside is outperforming your people (in which case, why not buy it from them?).

You should scrutinize capital allocation stringently. In principle, each project that is seeking capital should behave like a start-up, competing with all the other great ideas for the attention and backing of venture capitalists. If capital budgeting systems operated this way, then they'd perform like local capital markets instead of like political conventions.

Economics, not politics. Business, not organization. Build an ass-kicking culture, not an ass-kissing one. In the world of future wealth, everyone inside an organization is also outside, subject to marketplace forces. That's as it must be.

MOVE POWER TO THE PERIPHERY—AND BEYOND

Industrial technologies are concentrating ones. They thrive on economies of scale and require large supporting organizations. But organizations turn inward as they grow. Like a balloon when it is inflated, the internal volume increases much more rapidly than does the surface area, so the number of internal workers increases much more rapidly than does the number of those with direct marketplace contact.

As long ago as the 1980s, some corporations identified these problems and tried to cure them by breaking their organization into any number of small business units (SBUs). The smaller the organizational unit, the thinking went, the closer it would be to market forces. ABB (the Swiss-Swedish industrial giant now organized into more than 1,300 units), Corning (a U.S. glass maker), and Thermoelectron (a Waltham, Massachusetts, manufacturer of scientific, medical, and industrial instruments) were among those to steer by this star. In each example, the corporation bought more risk, and time will reveal the payoff.

Information technologies came along just in time to fuel these experiments. By their nature, such technologies are distributive, they don't require large scale, and they bring the outside world in. Now everyone—regardless of rank, location, or time—can have access to the same information. This flattens hierarchy and shifts power to the periphery.

This migration is not about to be stopped by a boundary that is crumbling as we speak. The more the connected infrastructure matures, the more power will migrate beyond the periphery, putting more of a company's decision-making power in nonemployees' hands. Already, customers not only dictate Toyota's production schedule but also submit their own list of options which they want the factory to build in. In 1997, Downes and Mui, in *Unleashing the Killer App*, recommended that leaders "outsource to the customer."[2]

Learning to change as fast as the marketplace means that customers are, in effect, designing your organization. When your organization changes as fast as your business, that's as it should be. What seems like the risk of reallocating your resources is really the opportunity to keep pace with the market. What feels like chaos is effective adaptation. *The firm is never firm.*

MARKETPLACE RULES FOR HUMAN CAPITAL

We haven't forgotten about the most valuable natural resource: human capital. It has a vital role in helping companies run by marketplace rules. Everyone in your organization can already post their résumé on Monster.com and find out how the market for their skills is doing each day. As Monster.com's CEO, Jeff Taylor, says, "Companies will stop posting most jobs and simply choose from among the résumés in the database."[3] Others will be auctioned off. We argued earlier that a company should allocate capital as though it were a venture capitalist betting on the most worthy risks. It will be the same with human capital.

If you run every other part of your business by marketplace rules, can you still treat your employees as if they had no other options? Of course not—that puts them all at risk. Your organization must offer each person the opportunity to maximize her human capital. You needn't offer a fat compensation package yet, but at least a prospectus for human capital growth.

THAT'S A WRAP

What's left for the traditional organization when a company operates like a cost-conscious Hollywood producer, assembling requisite resources as needed from the efficient marketplace? In one sense, a lot less. But what comes as a surprise to most companies is that they gain a lot more in speed and creativity. Allowing ideas and people to flow in and out of their organization is a lot less risky than keeping things secret, controlled, and out of sight of the competition. This understanding lies beneath the vibrant, high-frequency transformation and excitement of the Silicon Valley business culture. It is what John Kao advocates in *Jamming*.[4]

By taking this approach, a company ensures that, even inside the organization, it benefits from efficient markets—remember the Hewlett-Packard forecasting example. You're creating an organization in which each element has the incentive to adapt to its own marketplace, unimpeded by the politics and budgeting systems of the traditional bureaucracy. And the churn this creates will accelerate innovation.

Finally, it makes it easier to adapt the whole organization to changing times, because each unit is potentially self-sufficient. Even your most valued talent may move on—with your blessing. The producer doesn't give the cinematographer severance pay when the movie is wrapped.

The organizations of the twentieth century were built around concentrating technologies. The organizations of the twenty-first will be built around distributive ones. The Berlin Wall fell in 1989. Organizations aren't forever, but the more they let the outside in, the better their chances for survival.

Future Wealth Expectation: *By 2010, less than half the work performed in U.S. organizations will be done by full-time employees.*

FROM PAYROLLS TO PORTFOLIOS
Transforming Human Resource Management

At the 2010 Partnership Committee meeting of Staid, Static, and Stuck, Vice Chairman Hoover insisted that Alycia Fields should not be admitted to the partnership because of her abrasive manner. "Are you kidding?" countered the HR director. "Just look at what she's trading at."

ONE OF US remembers a senior vice president of human resources saying of his profession, "We are the conscience of the corporation. We stand for what is right and good. We are the ones who speak the truth, who can say that the king has no clothes, because we have an unspoken, unwritten, unconscious agreement with senior management that . . . we'll never win." That's quite an indictment.

If human resources, more accurately labeled "intellectual capital and knowledge workers," are the most important resource in business today, and if financial capital is less scarce than talent, then why is the human resource function less important than the finance function in most corporations?

The HR function gets lots of lip service about its importance, and it certainly has grown in significance since its name changed from "personnel" around two decades ago. Some companies have begun to increase the volume of rhetoric in recognition of this shift. Software maker Intuit, for instance, has appointed Barb Karlin as its "Director of Great People" to recruit and retain stellar, high-performing employees.[1] But while human resources has moved steadily to the fore, HR has still never quite made it into the center ring.

Could it involve the soft sciences of humans and the hard sciences attached to money and numbers? Even the best training and development practices in the corporation lag behind the maturity of financial accounting methods. Efforts to improve T&D within the existing framework are likely to creep forward only in increments. To accomplish more rapid improvements in managing human resources, we need a new paradigm, not a better implementation of the existing one.

HUMAN CAPITAL-BACKED SECURITIES

The marketplace, and not corporate HR departments, will present the new paradigm. In the preconnected economy, financial capital was the scarce resource. The market created a panoply of financial instruments to address this need. Today, intellectual capital is the scarce resource, and a host of financial instruments will emerge to help allocate it.

Financial institutions will set the pace in coming up with these instruments, just as mortgage-backed securities arose from the securities industry and not from the real estate industry. As more risks become interchangeable, creative people in the securities industry will manage to package and build markets to trade them. We think that human capital will be no exception.

HR departments are so internal to the organization—and so far removed from marketplace rules—that they are unlikely to create such vehicles. Far more likely, however, is another creative source, a new form of company that specializes in putting together buyers and sellers of intellectual capital.

In fact, future wealth offers a big opportunity for the head-hunters, agents, and even unions who already serve as intermediaries between companies and their employees and contract workers to reposition their business. They could form partnerships with the securities industry and help introduce the trading of human capital on an electronically efficient market. Two firms that are already taking very different approaches here are the well-established Manpower, Inc., and the new Web company Monster.com.

Manpower is the world's second-largest placer of temporary workers.[2] Once a pacesetter, it now seems hobbled by high overhead and insufficient focus on technical workers. The company may not be moving fast enough beyond yesteryear's model, working to deepen its relationship with the people it places. Manpower developed free agent human capital assets by providing its temps with benefits, coaching and advising them, and generally enhancing them for client companies. So far, this makes sense. When companies need financial capital, they turn to financial institutions. When they need human capital, they turn to institutions that provide it, such as Manpower. But the people Manpower places are becoming more like their own employees assigned to projects in client companies. The temps return to the parent for refreshers, further training, and redeployment. But rather than turn temps into employees, the company should start to use the electronic and financial technologies now available to build a more efficient marketplace for exchanging and trading them as human capital. *Somebody* will do it.

Meanwhile, Monster.com, cyberspace's job bulletin board, has become one of the hottest addresses on the Net. Monster offers job résumé management, a personal job search agent, a careers network, newsletters, and a "My Monster" customization feature for special requests and skills. As of November 1999, some 2.2 million résumés had found their way onto the Monster site. "We are like a big city" says CEO Jeff Taylor. "We provide an infrastructure of 82 million page views or 7.6 million visitors a month." Within two years, Taylor believes that Monster.com will have more than 10 million résumés in its database and will move from being a reactive short-term "needs" filler to being a proactive provider of skills.[3]

Recruiting is a $17 billion-a-year industry, and Forrester Research of Cambridge, Massachusetts, predicts that the on-line piece of the business, a mere $105 million in 1998, will reach $1.7 billion by 2003. Half the companies on *Fortune*'s Global 500 list already use the Web to find talent.[4] Among technology companies, the figure is probably much higher. It certainly is at Cisco Systems. According to *Fortune*, Cisco hires 61 percent of its people and receives 81 percent of its résumés via the Net.[5]

Monster.com and competitors such as CareerPath.com, Job-Search.com, and HotJobs.com use the Net mainly for their classified ads, because it saves time. Cisco's HR chief, Barbara Beck, told *Fortune* that recruiting on the Net has trimmed the number of days to fill a job from 113 to 45.[6]

These efforts mark the beginning of a more efficient labor market, where bids and counteroffers whirl back and forth as in any other true market exchange. Some job hunters are already seeing the benefits of more efficient markets, as would-be employers try to outbid each other at auctions for the talent they demand.

Many employees feel underrewarded by their company, of course, and that the only way up is out. Indeed, conventional wisdom holds that you can advance in both career and compensation only by hopping from one company to another. Now, imagine a world in which people anonymously post their current job descriptions and reward packages. Employers monitor the postings, making bids whenever they spot somebody they want who has an asking price they're willing to pay. Suppose somebody else wanted the same person? The market would determine the true value of these tradable assets.

Of course, this true market price will never be all it takes to sign on a smart new employee. If you think of "hiring" new workers, then you will get safe bets, not stars. If you think of "acquiring" them as you would a Picasso, then you will have a better chance of attracting intellectual capital to create future wealth.

Intellectual capital will never be the same as financial capital. It's not as liquid. You can't off-load workers as you would Korean bonds at the first sign of market trouble. Financial assets may need coddling, but they lack perishable flesh and feelings. Cash holds no grudges, makes no moral judgments, files no lawsuits. You must woo and win intellectual assets. Your corporate mission must move them personally. You must supplement such traditional obligations with a financial development of your employees' potential. This approach treats people with the respect that they deserve—and that they will increasingly not only demand but command. Usually, when employers think of people as assets, they do so mainly as metaphor. We are suggesting something much more literal, more like a talent agent or orchestra conductor, or coaches—like a Joe Torré or a Phil Jackson.

BUY BRAINS, NOT HEADCOUNT

When most companies try to control their costs, they start by cutting people on their payroll. But when labor—brain over brawn—becomes an asset to accumulate, you begin to think twice about throwing it away. Lay off risk, not talent. The actual number is relevant, naturally, but it is secondary to your people's intellectual output, determined not by market demand but by creative ability. More David Bowie and less David Cassidy; more Frank Sinatra, less Frankie Avalon.

Assembly lines need a certain body count to run well. But get the right software writer, and that one person is worth dozens, if not hundreds, of other workers, not only on the assembly lines but at both ends of the production cycle, too. When IBM bought Lotus, the deal clincher was Ray Ozzie, the designer of the best-selling Lotus Notes software, who agreed to remain as part of the package. Ray Ozzies are assets to grow, not resources to administer. Not all programmers have an equal asset value, but all should be treated according to the same rules.

Companies and their human resource directors also must reevaluate how they reimburse employees for continuing education. Today, most companies take an all-inclusive administrative approach, paying for the course if, say, the employee earns a grade of B or better and if the course relates to the employee's current job, not his or her aspirations or the corporate vision. The market-based approach takes a supply-and-demand attitude instead, saying, "We really need people who can program in C++ and not Visual Basic, so we will pay three times tuition for those who pass C++ and only 25 percent of the Visual Basic tuition." If you articulate and develop such a principle, then you'll achieve a finely tuned and graded scale that marries human asset development to market expectations and strategic directions. You may find it better, faster, and cheaper to post your need for C++ programmers on the Net and see how many come to you, already trained.

Measuring the output of human resources and putting a value on them is inherently difficult when the quality rather than the quantity of the work is what matters. Measuring quality, after all, is subjective. Performance reviews by supervisors rarely get close to providing constructive criticism. The so-called 360-degree reviews, where bosses and subordinates contribute to one's performance assessment, are more accurate but still fall short because they're still internal measures. An employee who tells her employer of other job offers with the not-so-subtle implication "Match it or I leave," however, is using market, not internal, logic. She's signaling her boss, "The market says I'm worth more than you're paying me."

Instead of resenting the pressure put on you to match a job offer your employee gets from a competing firm, learn to appreciate and profit from the feedback the market is giving you.

Most companies now have compensation frameworks that may do more harm than good. Because they define pay ranges for each function and level, they force-fit all of their employees into pigeon-holes. The consequence? Employees who leave are often the most valuable ones. We all know the pecking order—a supervisor must earn more than those supervised, even if the employees contribute more to the bottom line. Older employees tend to earn more than their younger peers, even if their work requires a lower level of energy and creativity. Women are still paid less than men for similar work.

Some jobs lend themselves well to performance measurement. Salespeople and investment bankers, among others, have numbers to prove their worth. Professional athletes are directly hooked to the markets. The $52 million over four years that the Arizona Diamondbacks agreed to pay strikeout king Randy Johnson reflected both the bidding war for Johnson's services and a cold-blooded calculation of how many extra fans the "Big Unit" could bring to the ballpark when he took the mound.[7]

Sometimes bidding wars reach the corporate suite, too. In June 1999, Joseph Galli, a former Black & Decker executive, signed an employment pact with PepsiCo to become chief executive of its Frito-Lay North America snack foods business. On June 24, Galli met with Pepsi's top executives at corporate headquarters in Purchase, New York. He even did a telephone interview with a reporter to discuss his Pepsi job. Within hours, Galli had a change of heart—

and another new job. Galli's lawyers informed Pepsi that night that he was heading, not for New York, but for Seattle, where he would become president and chief operating officer of Amazon.com.[8]

HOW TO EMPOWER HR–REALLY

Such bidding for talent is still more or less restricted to the upper ranks of a company and is unlikely to trickle down through a company for at least ten years. In the meantime, *why not establish a market price for each of your employees?* Headhunters, or for that matter the help wanted sections of professional journals, could provide estimates of the compensation range that each of your employees could expect out in the real world.

A company should securitize its best and brightest workers and let them float on the market themselves. We'll discuss this idea more fully in the next chapter. Securitization is not likely to be carried out under the HR flag, but by helping to lay the path in that direction, HR can show that it does not have to be an unempowered, internal, administrative part of a company. Instead, it can prove itself a powerful, wealth-creating driver that focuses on human capital. To do so, HR must transform itself from the internal and bureaucratic Ministry of Labor into a broker on the trading floor of the Human Capital Exchange.

Future Wealth Expectation: *Today's CVs and résumés will gradually yield to a more comprehensive and balanced statement of human capital assets and liabilities. Standardizing this information will facilitate human capital trading, as 10ks did for corporate stock trading.*

FROM VESTING TO INVESTING
Maximizing the Market Value of Your Human Capital

The Kron Corporation employs 50,000 people, of whom it has identified 1,000 as its future wealth. How can it keep and reward them accordingly? Kron could pay the Elite 1,000 far more than their peers, but that will dog the bottom line. Or offer them stock options, but the accounting benefits of that practice are threatened.

Kron told these people: "We recognize your value, so in addition to your binding yourself to us via an options plan, let us bind ourselves to you. Use our lawyers and our accountants to set yourselves up as companies of one, with our blessing and financial support. In return, you sell an option on 10 percent of your company-of-one paper to us. We'll bundle all the 10 percents that you and the other 999 smart cookies sell us and market them as a new security: the Kron Brain Trust. Instead of your becoming minority shareholders in us via a stock option plan that binds you, we'll become minority shareholders in you."

THE CONNECTED ECONOMY will create a more efficient labor market, and that market will determine the value of intellectual capital more accurately than the corporation does now. Underwriting intellectual capital and trading the risk of individuals' future performance could figure greatly both in companies' reward systems and in their future capital structures.

SECURITIZING TALENT

The Kron Corporation arrangement is a reward system that works in both directions. In addition to employees' investing in their company, the company invests in the future profit streams of its best people. Kron's two-way investment flow between individuals and companies allows each to take direct financial positions in the other.

Consistent with our theme, stock options emphasize assets over income and for a decade have been the most sought-after part of the compensation package. But they are a one-way play. With stock options, a company says, in effect, "We think so well of you that we'll let *you* invest in *us*."

By granting workers the right to buy stock in their company, at a future date at a set price, a company hopes to capture employee loyalty, motivate workers to achieve superior results so that the share price rises, and at the same time hyperreward them for their effort with a fat, down-the-road capital gain.

Conventional wisdom argues that loading up executives and even employees as a whole with options serves to align their interests with those of shareholders. From an economic point of view, talent may remain where it's unnecessary, just to cash in the options. From a corporate point of view, stock options are a valuable approach because they delay compensation and move debt off the books and into the future.

Under existing accounting practices, companies must reveal the effect that stock options would have had on earnings had they been treated as normal compensation. But they must do so only in foot- notes to their financial statement, terra incognita for the average investor. Pay Sanford Weill of Citigroup $50 million in salary, and the bank's bottom line will shrink $50 million. Grant him two mil- lion options, and he'll claim $50 million only if he ups the com- pany's performance so effectively that the stock rises $25.

Employees and companies both love stock options, with good reason. If the stock does well, then employees can get rich, a just return for investing their human capital in the company. If the stock price tanks, then workers might lose the salary forgone for options, but they suffer no out-of-pocket expenses. For an increasing num- ber, this risk-reward trade-off attracts talent. As for companies, if the company prospers and the stock does well, then options are an investment in the financial health and general morale of employees. If the company falters and the stock lags, then the options cost the company little. Meanwhile, workers will have been motivated to do their best, even if in a losing cause, and their incentives align with the company's objectives. By most means of reckoning, stock options are a trade that benefits both clubs.

Stock options hold onto key people but reduce the efficiency of the markets for human capital. A worker might create more value for the economy elsewhere, but her "golden handcuffs" keep her from moving.

LIFE AFTER OPTIONS

On the other hand, the assurance that valuable human capital can be retained has a beneficial effect. It encourages companies to invest in their people, spending money to round out their experience with international or cross-functional exposure, for example; supporting executive education; and even throwing in the occasional sabbatical. Some companies—GE and McKinsey, for example—are known as great places for people to be developed, a virtue they exploit when looking for talent.

Investing in the development of employees will become less attractive, obviously, when they become really mobile. Does this mobility mean even more stock options? Possibly, though proposed changes in accounting standards would require much clearer statements of what options really cost a company. That, to be sure, would make options less attractive to the companies that issue them.

But what if your company got a stake in you that paid off whether you left their employ or not? In effect, they'd receive a hedge against the risk of your leaving. This hedge would make your employer even more willing to invest in you. So the economy gets both greater investment in human capital and a more efficient human capital market.

Let's review Kron to see how wealth can flow in both directions. The valued employees have picked up the money that their company invested in them. Meanwhile, by marketing the Kron Brain Trust, the company could also have extra cash.

What does a company do with the proceeds from a Kron Brain Trust, or with the profits from the amalgamation of start-up companies funded? It might pay the salary and benefits of those talented 1,000 still on payroll. Alternatively, the company could include Brain Trust shares, or proceeds from them, in the matching funds it contributes to the employees' 401(k) plans. That way, everyone, from CEO to janitorial staff, would have a stake in the company's intellectual capital.

And why stop with investing in just the intellectual capital (IC) of your inside stakeholders? Why not invest also in the IC of your customers and suppliers and distributors? Any business is a loop, from concept to customer and onward to more conception. Why not invest in every station along the circle and help create a future wealth *keiretsu*? Nor is it only a matter of owning a share in your suppliers, hiring great employees, and "hiring" great customers, as many companies already do. How much wiser it would be to own a share in the brainpower, the creativity, of your suppliers, distributors, and customers. As the economy drives toward intangible value, intangibles increasingly influence every inch of the profit (or loss) stream.

OWN YOUR IDEAS

The Kron idea is pretty radical, and obviously it will take a while to figure out how to make it work. Another way to monetize intellectual capital would be to securitize the *idea* rather than the person who dreamed it up. Today, when engineers working for a corporation make new discoveries, they might be rewarded with bonuses or stock options, but the key resource, the patent, goes to the employer. Companies understandably want to protect their investment in research and development, but doing so minimizes the upside for the talent. There is no incentive for engineers to keep discovering things if each idea is stripped from them as soon as it proves its utility.

Suppose a company announced that it would require the right of first refusal on whatever patents its employees secured—not first refusal on the discovery itself, but on funding whatever business the discovery might spawn. Maybe the company would want to decline the opportunity. Even great ideas sometimes don't fit with corporate missions. If the company did become a partner with the inventors, it would be investing in the intellectual capital of its employees, instead of requiring its employees to invest in the company to realize their greatest reward.

This approach would help combat the averaging that is imposed on companies by most human resource systems, and it would offer individuals a higher risk-reward compensation option. Maybe you don't have the confidence to go out and start a venture with your e-gizmo, but you'd be happy to put 15 percent of your salary on the line to have it funded because you'd receive a chunk of its equity. You'd have managed the business risk to fit your own risk profile.

Even if a corporation has chosen and nurtured its employees well, they will nevertheless eventually leave. Efficient markets rarely take no for an answer. So why not structure an arrangement that motivates them to stay, while giving the enterprise a hand in their future profit streams?

A company could invest in the person's ability to create. This is the opposite of depreciating assets. Rather than depreciate on the books, you can appreciate in the market. In effect, it's unbundling a worker's intellectual capital from his or her flesh-and-blood capital. Think of the money the company puts up as a start-up loan and often as a guarantee of that critical first customer for the eventual product, rather than as equity.

It's already begun—First Yale created a student loan program in which repayment requirements depended on the individual's financial success. More recently, business schools have begun to invest in their students. Columbia, Michigan, Northwestern, NYU, and UCLA have each started venture capital funds to take positions in some of their full-time MBAs' entrepreneurial start-ups. Columbia invested $250,000 in a New York winery, and Northwestern put $150,000 into three companies, including a market research and sports marketing firm, each started by a graduating student. Profits from most of these investments go back into their respective funds to invest in more student entrepreneurs.[1]

Whether schools or businesses, students or staff are involved, trading risks benefits both parties. And in truth it is only a small leap from investing in such ideas to investing directly in the people who have them. You have two investment opportunities: (1) the idea in the intellectual property and (2) the person (human capital) who created it. Separate the risks and invest in both. Companies must determine which asset they manage best, the idea or the person.

THE END OF THE OPTIONS OPTION?

Compare investing in people's ideas to investing in stock options. Options and other golden handcuffs are attempts to circumvent efficient human capital markets by restricting the movement of talent. The investment approach does just the opposite, offering individuals a broader range of choices while cutting their investors— the corporations who have helped to develop the human assets—in on the potential upside of the deal. This arrangement differs from a retainer because the value is not fixed and immovable.

The question of stock options will soon become more than theoretical. The Financial Accounting Standards Board (FASB), the Supreme Court of the accounting profession, is soon likely to put limits on the tax advantages that current options bookkeeping make possible.

Twice in recent years, FASB, urged on by various shareholder activist groups, has attempted to rein in what it sees as the excesses of stock option plans. FASB is examining "repricing," the practice of reducing the "strike price" at which employees can exercise their options to buy shares if the stock falls. Apple Computer, Bay Networks, Oracle, Best Buy, Oxford Health Plans, and Netscape Communications (since bought by AOL) were among the companies that adopted repricing programs during the 1999 slide in high-tech stocks.[2]

What happened at Netscape illustrates why repricing so incenses ordinary shareholders. After its price crashed, the board authorized a repricing program for some 8.6 million options it had granted to a new strike price: $16.81. Shortly thereafter, Netscape's stock soared to $30.88. The repriced shares were now worth an extra $121 million.[3] This gain ultimately came at the expense of the outside shareholders. Further, if Netscape had treated that $121 million as a compensation expense, it would have reduced Netscape's 1997 gross profit by almost 27 percent. And that, in fact, is exactly what FASB is proposing that companies must do. Not surprisingly, companies have been resisting. Stock options, of course, are future wealth–friendly. They allow temporarily slumping companies to stay competitive in the fierce battle for talent.

Greg Maffei, Microsoft's CFO, makes the essential point "Microsoft needs its software people more than it needs its shareholders. In some senses, outside shareholders exist to monetize employee stock options."[4] If and when stock options do disappear, or decrease, as a way to bid for talent, the next play will involve corporations' making direct investments in their best human talent. In its quest to add value to pay, business will turn to the fastest growing asset and the one thus far least tapped as a source of compensation. We think the answer is: *monetizing brain power and leveraging its future worth in the financial marketplace.*

MONETIZING HUMAN CAPITAL

A fund of start-up individuals or ventures? Securitizing the ideas or the people who have the ideas? Look at the two sides of the equation long enough, and they begin to morph into one another. Either way (and there are surely others as well), the main point is that business is figuring out how to monetize and trade intellectual capital.

The nature of the risk instruments is far from clear, and we have little experience managing their peculiar risks. Today's gifted, hard-charging employees could be tomorrow's dropouts or burnouts. Are they obligated to buy back their own paper? What if they've spent everything? Do you write them off as bad debt? Sell them at a loss?

A first step in this surely gradual evolution might be to take a lesson from the corporate raiders of the 1980s. They saw the flawed valuation system of financial accounting, in which a company's book value represents the net value of its parts. Thus, a highly profitable unit disguises the failures of a loser, for example, and efficiencies cover up inefficiencies. A company might own valuable real estate, but that could be offset by dilapidated equipment. Raiders took the assets apart and were able to profit by salvaging the losers as best they could, while allowing the winners to thrive.

In practice, raiders who gained control of a company were the exception. Most found their real profits in greenmail, the premiums that companies paid to the raiders beyond the price of the shares they had amassed. But the raiders preached a good lesson: To find true value, unbundle various parts of a company and let each float in the marketplace. Why shouldn't one of the unbundled units be the company's intellectual capital? Almost certainly, its rising value has been supporting collapsing worth elsewhere in the organization.

Suppose that General Motors divided itself into three businesses: (1) the assets of GM Manufacturing, the factories that make its parts, cars, and trucks; (2) GM Finance, which makes the customer loans and finances the leases; and (3) what we'll call "GM Brain Trust," an entity that owns a part of the cash flows of the designers, top managers, export whizzes, research scientists, computer system architects, and other top talent.

GM's plant and equipment has been extensively and expensively updated in the last decade. On the other hand, the stock market has been devaluing traditional manufacturing capabilities. But GM Manufacturing would be free to pursue manufacturing business around the world, in addition to working for GM. Would its price-earnings ratio exceed that of GM today?

GM Finance is today the most profitable part of the business. We suppose that, unbundled from the lower-performing assets, the division's market cap would rise. And what of GM Brain Trust? This group of very talented people would be free to put themselves to use inside the GM business—or elsewhere. Given the market's perception that GM's value is dragged down by its layers of bureaucracy, the market might see real potential in this risk, and bid Brain up.

By unbundling the company, the market would be continuously measuring, not the corporation as a whole, but its core parts. Separating your most valuable asset, human capital, from the rest could set off a chain reaction, and all asset groups—physical, financial, and human—might unbundle. If this happened, each group would be valued according to the market's estimate of its unique worth, rather than being averaged and perhaps distorted.

Once again, events have overtaken our expectations. On 2 November 1999 both Ford and GM announced that all purchasing would have to be conducted on-line. Ford's portal AutoXchange and GM's MarketSite will connect all the companies' suppliers, partners, and customers worldwide. AutoXchange will be partnered with Oracle and brought public fairly soon. Tellingly, GM intends to keep its portal internal. "It may not be crazy to imagine AutoXchange being worth as much as the traditional businesses of its parents," reported *The Economist*. "Before too long both Ford and GM should be able to make cars in the same way as Dell makes computers—each built to order and delivered within a few days. They may even realize that they no longer need to make cars at all, deciding to follow the example of Cisco Systems, a data-networking firm, by becoming virtual companies whose expertise lies in design and brand marketing."[5]

Would unbundled companies have a higher market capitalization than their bundled predecessors? Value has been migrating steadily toward intangible assets and, as we have said, no asset is more intangible and more valuable than intellectual capital. Either way, whether the aggregate unbundled stock was worth more or less than the bundled one, the market measure of worth would be more true. The market, after all, would base its valuation on more discrete information, delivered in real time, on more particular elements of the company. Welcome to the future wealth of electronic markets for packaging, investing, and trading in human capital.

Future Wealth Expectation: *The financial services industry will develop mutual funds to hold people-backed securities.*

12

FROM PAST TO FUTURE
Measures That Matter

A virtual close is the ability to close the financial books with a one-hour notice.

— JOHN CHAMBERS, CEO, Cisco Systems

MEASURE THE FUTURE

Professional investors will tell you immediately that the way they value a company is to look at its future—specifically at the discounted future cash flows—and they do so all the time. A company should take the same approach, in looking not only at itself but also at everything that impacts it, including competitors, suppliers, customers, and the business it does.

Now that we're accustomed to paying $100 a share for Internet start-ups that don't anticipate profits this side of Judgment Day, the future orientation seems obvious. Yet the systems that companies use to measure and manage their performance are still locked onto the rearview mirror.

In part, they're prisoners of their auditors, and if you use the same measure, you, too, will value a company by what it has amassed in the past. Value it by income, as security analysts do, and you are valuing it close to the present. Value a company by its growth potential—where it is going and at what rate of acceleration—as venture capitalists do, and you are valuing it on its future. You're also taking a greater risk. But remember, in future wealth, risk is a good word. No wonder the most hotly desired companies in today's markets, those with the highest price-earnings ratios, are the likes of Amazon, Yahoo! and eBay.

The enormous multiples that these fly-by-tomorrow-night companies enjoy infuriate the disciplined managers who consistently generate strings of single-digit quarterly earnings increases at the thirty companies that comprise the Dow Jones Industrial Average. They learned to believe that managing current performance creates value, but now investors are parting ways with this dogma. They place much greater value on promising future markets.

Companies need to make the same mind-set adjustment. This means that their perception of the future—its direction, its opportunities—should dictate how they manage. In every corporation we have seen, such perceptions are discounted because the information on which they are based is uncertain. To bet your capital on uncertainties would surely be seen as overly risky at some of the Dow companies. That's why their capital budgeting systems are designed to present returns as if they were certain.

MEASURE INTANGIBLES

Not surprisingly, corporate measurement systems are based largely on what you can see: units in inventory, number of customers, bills payable, the replacement cost of a drill press, bank debt, the age of a steel mill, dollars. When the auditors prepare a balance sheet, they put a value on what they can count. But how do you count brand, capacity to innovate, quality of management, potential, relationships, knowledge, human capital?

Some answers are beginning to emerge. Companies are beginning to get a handle, for example, on the value of their brands. Sophisticated market research techniques allow the likes of Bell Atlantic and MicroAge to learn just how much more—or less—a given product is worth if it carries their name. This can be substantial. "I'd like to buy the world a cola" doesn't have the same selling power as the branded, "I'd like to buy the world a Coke." At the other extreme, we know of no means of putting a value on relationships, though researchers are beginning to codify and quantify social networks. But we do know they have value because, without them, a company fails.

Even if you can't yet measure all intangibles directly, the financial analysts have an implicit model that places value on them. Ernst & Young research shows that, on average, nonfinancial performance accounts for 35 percent of analysts' valuations.[1] If you want to know where you are over- and underinvesting in intangibles, go ask those efficient financial markets. They'll always find a way to take account of all available information and set a value on it. It's an indirect feedback loop, but the most comprehensive one you've got. In the future, companies may produce simulation models of their markets to measure their intangibles.

Three things here: It's no secret that intangibles are growing faster than tangibles. How to measure their value is still elusive. And third, the financial markets will figure a way.

MEASURE CONTINUOUSLY

One thing about measuring is very certain. It needs to be continuous. How often do you close the books, upgrade products, change prices, deliver or receive performance reviews, and the like—periodically, quarterly, semiannually, yearly? In each case, moreover, the measurements and the changes are likely to be at the tail end of a drawn-out cycle that begins with the gathering of information, its analysis, endless discussion and committee work, and often-ponderous executive decision making. Then come roll-out, response, results, and more fine-tuning. And, of course, once you finally reach the end of the cycle, you must begin it again.

Contrast this with financial markets, where the price of a stock can change in the space of a busy signal while you're calling your broker, and where whole sectors can tumble into near dust while you sleep. Such constant fluctuation remains the extreme, but we are all becoming accustomed to a world, in business and otherwise, in which connectivity-driven change is nearly continuous. It's reflected in spot pricing, once the arcane domain of oil traders and other commodity traders and now a part of everybody's life. It's almost bad etiquette these days to ask the person next to you on an airline what he paid for his seat. The carriers change prices faster than you can figure out whether to even make the trip. Only those willing to pay a premium for the intangible value of complete flexibility pay full sticker price.

Continuous measurement is the way manufacturers control machinery. Since the 1970s, they have been installing real-time measurement and control systems to increase productivity and quality and to reduce labor costs. This same logic is inching into the intangible sector. Programmed trading and various circuit breakers are sensing devices. But they are reactive and limited. If we could install continual measurement and control systems in the intangible parts of our business, then we would also benefit from speed of reaction, improved quality, and greater productivity. We'd also gain a set of tools that would help us manage risk. A stop-loss order controls the risk of losing money in a given security. What is the real-time intangible equivalent? If Sears had created a brand value measurement system in the 1960s, it could have reacted a lot quicker.

The movie industry comes close to continuous measurement. Always given to dailies—the end-of-the-day feedback loop for the director—studios now monitor the theater grosses every morning and make instant advertising and distribution decisions. Electrical utilities plug into on-line auctions for power, cruising North American and European grids and making real-time pricing decisions.

For continuous measurement, you first must increase the frequency of your traditional accounting-based measures. Cash flow, profits, and the rest obviously continue to matter—no point planning for tomorrow if you haven't got a pulse today. How much longer, though, before the quarterly numbers become what annual statements already are: little more than archival documents? And how long will it be before weekly, daily, and even moment-by-moment numbers evolve providing continual market feedback? Cisco Systems has already announced that it will be closing its books daily. Wal-Mart provides profit-and-loss numbers to department mangers at the close of business each night.[2] Right there you have a vision of future wealth accounting.

Today's software and local area networks provide continuous measurement, but only within an organization. In the real dimension, process industries such as chemicals and paper rely on instant measurement and real-time control systems to optimize their operations, but have no such infrastructure for managing wealth. The financial sector comes closer, because risk and the financial markets are their primary concern. Even so, no bank today can, say, close its books in real time. Continuous measurement requires electronic connectivity outside the enterprise—to customers, suppliers, and markets. Only then can we begin to manage wealth in real time.

Public schools, for example, have long divided the academic year into arbitrary grading periods and deliver measurements to parents every six to ten weeks. But just as an annual corporate report has almost no meaning to serious investors—the information is ancient history—so a child's grade that is based in part on a failed test taken ten weeks earlier is of little value to either a student or a parent. A ninth grader is only 728 weeks old himself, so a 10-week-old grade reflects how he or she did 1.4 percent of a lifetime ago. If you're 50 years old, 1.4 percent of your life would be 36 weeks ago, a long time for recriminations or praise (though not unheard of in many organizations!).

Imagine, though, a school where test grades are entered, not in a ring-binder gradebook, but on a teacher's ThinkPad, and from there transferred at the speed of light to a student's Personal Data Bank (PDB) account. Absences and late days would go into the same account, along with commendations, referrals to the principal's office, and anything else that might help paint a real-time portrait of a student's academic and social progress. Parents would be given a PIN number so they could use their own computers to access their children's PDB account at any time. Yes, moms and dads could become awfully intrusive in their children's life and in the affairs of the school. But then one of the points of continuous measurement is that it enables you to meddle or, to put it positively, to fine-tune continuously.

Measurements that are continuous, intangible, and future-oriented are essential underpinnings of future wealth. While this sounds a little like hearing the update of a hurricane warning every hour, the upside is the end of the tyranny of budgets that don't improve decision making and a relaxation of financial markets' overreactions to quarterly earnings. Since the ability to form a more robust and credible picture of the future distinguishes primates from lower mammals, perhaps it will help homo economicus reach a more balanced society.

Future Wealth Expectation: *Business performance measurement systems will become continual, future-oriented, and two parts intangible, one part tangible.*

PART IV

society

BALANCING FREEDOM AND ORDER has always embroiled society in political and ethical risk. Freedom feeds the creative spirit of entrepreneurs and tyrants alike. Order yields safe streets and land mines. As economies change, societies must adapt to maintain civil equilibrium.

To begin with, society must encourage risk taking by stringing safety nets for the risk takers—the borrowers and the lenders—who will invariably tumble from the high wire. This net needs careful setting. Too soft a landing means no risk, no reward, no future wealth. A back breaker means no takers.

Society must also recast many of its laws, particularly those governing bankruptcy, taxation, and social insurance. Future wealth is a democratic force. As it flows from the traditional few into the growing middle class, it will economically emancipate as neither Karl Marx nor America's Founding Fathers ever imagined. The new wealthy and those who realize their own human capital potential will demand wealth-friendly laws. Will lawmakers take these steps? Politicians, like investors, can feel the direction of the wind.

13

FROM MARX TO MARKETS
Creating Middle-Class Wealth

Workers of the world unite.
The capital markets will set you free.

THE SHEER BREADTH of ownership of equities in U.S. society today has democratized wealth. According to the Federal Reserve, American households now control, either directly or through mutual funds, 59 percent of all stocks held in the United States, a staggering $9 trillion as of the end of summer 1999. Stocks accounted for only 12 percent of household financial assets in 1990, but 21 percent by 1999.[1]

"America's mutual funds are now worth more than either its pensions funds or its insurers, and are poised to overtake banks as the biggest repository of the nation's wealth," *The Economist* wrote in 1997.[2] Similarly, in 1998, the *Wall Street Journal* noted that this "phenomenal growth, combined with the flexibility and transparency that mutual funds offer, has given individual investors unprecedented control over America's finance industry."

Another indicator of important directional change is the 1992 Federal Reserve Survey of Consumer Finances, which found that about 22 percent of all equities belonged to people under the age of forty-five. That's practically double the ownership of a decade earlier.

MARX MANQUÉ

What businesses call "profits," economists call "surplus." When an economy creates surplus by making something for less than someone will pay for it, the society somehow gives some share of it to the owner of capital and some to labor. In the early twentieth century, as industrial technologies began creating great gobs of surplus in an economy with abundant labor and scarce capital, those who owned banks and big businesses began getting the lion's share of the wealth.

Enter Karl Marx with a relatively simple proposition: Owners and workers resembled masters and slaves, and the separation between the two would lead inevitably to a one-sided concentration of wealth and a plutocratic economic system. The broad mass of labor that built the pyramid would always bear the load, not the lucre. Marx argued to reintegrate worker and owner, giving the people control of the means of production, taking property out of private hands and giving it to the state. In a democratic society, all the people would share property of the state.

Marx's theories fell to Leninism, Maoism, Stalinism, Nazism, and *perestroika*. Far from dispersion among the people, power and wealth under these systems converged in the ruthless hands of the state and its bureaucrats. But the corruption of the theory didn't necessarily disprove the underlying thinking.

As early as the 1920s, many others in the industrialized world tried to redress the same social and political problems of economic disintegration and the growing wealth gap between owners and workers. Through the trade union movement, workers sought a collective voice to balance the power of the owner class and to bring their adversaries to the bargaining table. As unions gained strength, the share of surplus that flowed to labor grew. Remember, though, that many owners who viewed powerful labor as a threat to private property fiercely resisted unions in the United States.

The union movement could not have succeeded without the ballot box. Where democracy held sway, voters and their representatives consistently used nonrevolutionary political means to pursue equitable economic ends. In the United States, the progressive income tax, estate and capital gains taxes, and social security began to redistribute the fruits of ownership. Today, the Employee Retirement Income Security Act (ERISA), the ingenuity of the financial markets, and the arrival of the connected economy all broaden and deepen ownership. Financiers are freeing today's working class through a portfolio of equity investments in productive private companies.

A century ago, capital was a scarcer resource than land or labor. Today, the scarce resource is talent—intellectual capital, not financial capital—and information technology is the means of production most likely to create wealth. Neither is capital intensive. A few talented people can create a lot of value with a very affordable amount of information technology. One result could be a tremendous accelerator of economic development in the underdeveloped world. Another will be the redistribution of power in the developed one.

In an autocracy, despots abuse or suppress talent, whereas in a meritocracy, talent roams free and can rise to the top. In a plutocracy, robber barons exploit ideas, but in a democracy, the idea itself has worth, and its owner can convert it to product and broadly distribute it at a relatively low cost. That's where we are today.

In a democratic market economy, all of us already own our own intellectual capital. It's our private property from the get-go. This didn't matter too much to the ditchdigger of 1900, but is crucial as knowledge workers become more important. As companies of one, individuals hold their own capital assets. As ever, of course, talent is unevenly distributed across individuals. But the efficient human capital markets enable the talented to find their best use and hold on to their fair share.

Entrepreneurs lead the way, especially in Silicon Valley, where fortunes are made almost overnight. When these billionaires turn philanthropic, they invest in social capital, as did the Rockefellers, Carnegies, and Mellons.

The bigger story involves not the creation of wealth by the growing new entrepreneurial class, but the distribution of wealth. As we've grown richer, we've begun to save more, first investing in homes and now accumulating financial assets. Uncle Sam helped with tax breaks, subsidized loans, and legislation establishing tax-favored pension vehicles, such as 401(k)s and Keogh plans.

The disparity between the top and the bottom 10 percent may distract you from the 80 percent in the middle. Look closely: Median family income has grown a little more than 1.5 percent annually. Despite complaints in the 1980s of a stagnating middle class, family income grew in constant 1997 dollars from $20,102 in 1947 to $44,568 in 1997.[3] This income is being turned into financial wealth. Pensions have migrated to automatically vested contribution plans, which individuals keep with them as rollovers when they change jobs. Stock options spread ownership of the means of production ever more broadly, particularly in knowledge-intensive areas such as Silicon Valley.

Instead of separating workers and owners, the connected infrastructure and the financial sector of the economy are aligning the interests of enterprises and their employees—who *are* increasingly the owners. At the same time, 401(k) and other wealth-generating plans are aligning workers' interests with the interests of the whole economy. Furthermore, legislation altered distribution, and the capital markets are doing so even more.

Capital markets create equity, not equality. When the capital markets make ownership and wealth from intellectual capital, and when those financial assets reside in the individual, however, then the balance begins to tip toward larger numbers of people. When that happens, instead of concentrating at the top, wealth begins to spread broadly through the ranks. It just may be that capital markets distribute wealth more equitably than anyone previously imagined possible.

THE SUPER RICH ARE IRRELEVANT

"If all the superrich disappeared, the world economy would not even notice. The superrich are irrelevant to the economy," Peter Drucker said in *Forbes* in 1997. "The combined sources of money from retail investors, pension funds and retirement plans of all individuals is the fastest-growing source of money. The most important source of capital is the average mutual fund transaction of $10,000."[4] Drucker elaborated his point in *Wired* the next year. "The rich no longer matter," he said. "They're celebrities, not capitalists anymore. The real capitalists are the middle-class people who put $25,000 into a mutual fund."[5]

The only money Andrew Carnegie's employees saw was their wages, and few owned any stock. In contrast, Bill Gates has made an estimated one-third of Microsoft's 30,000 employees millionaires through the company's employee stock option plans. In his 1996 book, *The Road Ahead*, Gates said that one of the purposes of going public in 1986 was "to provide liquidity for the employees who had been given stock options."[6] The cars and housing prices around the company's hometown of Redmond, outside Seattle, showcase the shifting balance between income and financial assets, but not as clearly as this remark of Roxanna Frost, leadership manager at Microsoft: "We speak at Microsoft of the day when an employee calls in rich."[7]

A BETTER WAY TO MOTIVATE

If one company can produce 10,000 millionaires, then could 1,000 companies come up with 100 different ways to make 10 million millionaires? Probably not, because most companies aren't as pivotal to pioneering a new world as Microsoft has been. But suppose that the *Fortune* 1000 undertook the challenge to enhance the net worth of their employees—50 to 100 might succeed, and another 100 to 200 might have partial success. Along the way, they could all become laboratories of new and unique approaches to wealth creation and distribution.

Even though other companies do pursue the Microsoft way of distributing stock, most corporations, particularly large ones, still prefer to hold the bulk of stock options for the CEO and a few other select executives. They reward the majority of their employees primarily with a salary. Then they spend hundreds of millions of dollars on motivational programs. A much better idea: Align the interests of owners and employees, reward the best workers sufficiently that they begin to think like entrepreneur-owners, give them a stake in the whole and not just a bone from the part, through employee stock option plans and other increasingly popular stock purchase programs.

The gap between haves and have nots remains all too real. Wealth is pooling at the top alarmingly, and not every distribution of wealth will trickle down to those who need it most, in the United States or around the world. Still, control of wealth steadily migrates to a broader number of individuals. *An intangible knowledge economy is inherently more democratic than an economy based on tangibles, because ownership of the scarce resource is in the hands of the individual*. It's still true that brains are unequally distributed, as is access to educational facilities where minds can be trained and broadened. But we can take encouragement from some innovations. The capital markets are finding ways to help democracy work.

NARROWING THE GAP WITH MICROLENDING

The Internet community's 1999 INET conference in San Diego, where rich-country interests vied with poor-country concerns, highlighted these issues. Africa, with 13 percent of the world's population, has just 1 percent of the world's Internet users.[8] The gap in access to capital is now about access to intellectual capital.

How do you close or even narrow the gap when, worldwide, not one person in a hundred has a computer? By building relative wealth. Even the super poor can mobilize a financial net worth. However minuscule, microlending programs of various forms provide both financial and human capital to those who most need it around the world. A woman in Bangladesh who raised chickens borrowed enough to rent a cellular phone so that she could check chicken prices in neighboring villages. She evolved into a local telecom provider, earning twice the average wage, and her livestock became a profitable sideline.[9] "Give a man a fish, and he eats for a day." These programs teach people to fish, and they eat for a lifetime.

A number of groups, including the International Labor Organization (ILO), a UN agency based in Geneva, sent missions to Colombia, Iran, the Philippines, and other countries to study employment growth in the "sandal economy." The idea was to start with small capitalizations and, in the words of Hla Myint, a Burmese economist at the London School of Economics, to "let the market work."[10]

Compared to traditional economic development assistance, this meant betting less on central planning and constant top-down control, and more on market-supervised, bottom-up entrepreneurship.

It also came to mean spreading risk through offering microcredit, often only a fistful of dollars at a time, to any number of individuals. Significantly, it also meant a change in viewpoint. These programs looked at the poor who benefited from these economic initiatives as nascent businesses rather than as disguised underemployment.

If a peasant woman in India prepared hot food at home and brought it to her husband at work, then the ILO encouraged her to cook for a few more workers as a service business. The ILO oriented those who developed a small enterprise to hire one or more others. What began as a job growth strategy became microbusiness growth, with jobs and wages as outcomes.

By themselves, microcredit programs and the resulting enterprises obviously don't turn poor countries into rich ones. Judged by the criteria of financial lending, however, they have been successful: More than 90 percent of borrowers paid their loans.[11] The Grameen Bank in Bangladesh launched its first microcredit program 20 years ago and now enjoys a repayment rate of over 95 percent on more than $2.4 billion in loans. Grameen makes a profit on microlending.[12] Pressure from borrowers helps. The microentrepreneurs are clustered in small communities to create both mutual support and powerful peer pressure. Default on your loan and you freeze the credit of everyone else in the group. The borrowers form a kind of risk-taking commune.

By the late 1990s, microcredit programs had reached 15 million people living on a dollar a day or less, the poverty line as defined by the World Bank. Of those people, 13 million live in Asia.[13] Microcredit leaders have established the ambitious global goal of reaching 100 million people by 2005, still only a fraction of the planet's 1.6 billion impoverished people. To reach that target, moreover, the would-be lenders will have to expand dramatically into Africa, where only about 1.2 million of the estimated 300 million now living in poverty are currently in microcredit programs.

The poor are often suspicious of taking on debt, but it is risk aversion that often stands in the way of wealth creation in poor countries and rich. Although microcredit programs could reach many more borrowers, a great number stay away from debt, forgoing the risk—and the potential rewards.

In Chile, for example, capital markets support social innovations ranging from micro-lending to 401(k) plans to government-sponsored investment programs. Nations engage the energy and contribution of poor and not-so-poor alike, when they put surplus in people's hands through the capital markets rather than the state.

Future Wealth Expectation: *The growth of retail capital markets will accelerate economic development globally—and might even reduce the gap between haves and have-nots.*

FROM DEBTORS' PRISON TO CHAPTER 11
Higher Wires, Stronger Nets

In the first test of the Federal Bankruptcy Assistance Act (FBA), Judge Cline found that the Jaggi Trading Company was not eligible for the FBA "Get Back on Your Feet" loan. Jaggi's import-export business qualified as a "productive risk bearer" and an "economic benefit to society," the Judge said. But its foreign currency arbitrage far exceeded the hedging requirements of the business and constituted "speculative risk for which the Act offers no protection." Jaggi declared Chapter 11 bankruptcy.

IF THE FINANCIAL SERVICES industry creates integrated risk management accounts for individuals, how might society manage the risks of its citizens on an integrated basis? Perhaps, rather than all the point solution programs and tax codes we have today, we could legislate a kind of all-risks policy, rather like what Reliance has developed for corporate operating earnings, to cover every citizen.

When people view risk as a threat to wealth accumulation, public policy can help change the nation's mind. Consumption taxes, for example, prompt people to invest rather than consume their wealth. Higher capital gains taxes discourage people from churning their portfolios, hopefully reducing price speculation in favor of more moderate long-term risks. Bankruptcy laws provide some safety net without overly reducing the disincentive to take risks. And unions can push for labor contracts to put compensation at risk in exchange for sharing in productivity gains.

When a population takes risks to create wealth, society's institutions adjust. This is where public policy comes in. Social insurance programs, laws and regulations, and our tax system all need adjustment. Here are some speculations.

SOCIAL INSURANCE

The first modern social insurance program belonged to Bismarck's nineteenth-century Germany. Its architects designed it for those over sixty-five at a time when few survived that age. Other European nations followed suit. The U.S. government provided a form of social insurance as early as 1908, when it enacted a workman's compensation law, but the law extended only to federal employees performing hazardous work. Similar protection was extended next to U.S. railroad employees. Then came the widespread unemployment and bank collapses of the late 1920s and 1930s.

The Great Depression profoundly affected American attitudes toward risk, and a federally controlled and administered social insurance program was born almost overnight. The Social Security Act of 1935 extended protection against living too long—as life insurance protects against living too short—to most Americans. By the midpoint of the Information Age, the developed Western countries expected a safety net for citizens: Government must provide unemployment insurance for those out of work, social security for those with no savings, Medicaid for the elderly. The private sector offered insurance policies, with coverage against premature death, old age, fire and theft, disability—all downside risks.

In the early 1970s, a succession of private pension plans failed. Some had been looted. More had been closed down quite legally, when the sponsoring businesses failed. A number of retired workers who found themselves suddenly impoverished committed suicide. All this scandal or abuse led to the Employee Retirement Income Security Act (ERISA) of 1974, which required corporations to vest employees in their accrued pension plans before they reached retirement age. ERISA helped fund some employees' upside risks as well, by offering tax breaks. This law proved to be the fountainhead of the IRAs and 401(k) plans that then fueled the mutual fund industry.

If we believe that individuals should manage their real, financial, and human capital risks as an integrated whole, then we should expect governments to do the same for the population. And, in fact, workers' compensation, federal disaster assistance, and other programs do cover real risks. Social security and ERISA cover financial risks, and unemployment insurance deals with human capital risk. Here's how we might reorient two of our most controversial—social security and health care insurance—by managing risks as a portfolio.

SOCIAL SECURITY

Social Security in the United States is a pay-as-you-go system, not a funded retirement account. Workers and their employers pay social security taxes, almost all of which go immediately to current beneficiaries. The little that is left over goes into the system's trust fund. In 1998, the system collected $489 billion and paid out $382 billion, almost 80 percent. The remaining $107 billion went into the trust fund, which at the end of 1998 totaled $763 billion, just about enough to cover two years' worth of social security payments at current rates.[1]

Within thirty years, the aging of the population will reduce the number of workers per retiree by more than 30 percent, from about 3:1 today to about 2:1.[2] As the ratio of workers to beneficiaries shrinks, payments will exceed receipts, the trust fund will shrink, and the system will tank. Quite apart from many legitimate objections about political interference in the private economy, the much-discussed proposal to invest the trust fund in corporate equities would have little effect, because the annual benefit payouts dwarf the trust fund itself.

The state pension system of Chile, often cited as the best alternative to the U.S. social security system, is built on this investment model and has been copied by Argentina, Mexico, and Peru. In Chile, employees contribute 10 percent of their earnings into their own private retirement accounts, deductible from taxable income. Workers can choose among twenty private funds and change funds whenever they like. At retirement, individuals choose between either assuming the management of their savings or using them to purchase an annuity. The system encourages savings, which have increased an impressive 28 percent. The government guarantees a subsistence minimum for those who fail to save enough.[3]

President Clinton has proposed the notion of private investment accounts as part of the answer. Chile's approach can work from a standing start, before entitlements are established. But the United States cannot simply shift contributions from the trust fund to individual accounts to pay out in the future because there would be no money to fund current benefits.

But the idea of federally assisted investment accounts can be part of the solution. In *The Economist*, Martin Feldstein, the Harvard economist who was until recently director of the National

Bureau of Economic Research, noted that keeping benefits at their current levels would require a big hike in the social security payroll tax, from its current 12.4 percent to more than 19 percent. Pointing to the forecast for budget surpluses over the next twenty-five years, he made a relatively simple proposal: Create a mixed system, combining the existing pay-as-you-go payments with an investment plan. The government would deposit about 2.3 percent of your salary (up to the social security taxable maximum, currently $72,600) into your personal retirement account (PRA). You would then be able to select a fund manager, or the government could open an account for you with a private manager. When you reached retirement, you'd use your PRA balance to buy an annuity. You'd receive both the traditional tax-financed social security payment and the investment-funded PRA annuity. The government would guarantee this combination to be at least as large as the benefit you'd get under current law. Given current population projections, this change would sufficiently guarantee the current level of benefits forever.[4]

In an age of budget surpluses, this approach seems almost irresistible. If adopted as public policy, it would push the average level of risk in the society upward, by increasing the flow of funds to equity markets, lowering the cost of capital, and creating greater wealth. Further, it would apply to a very broad base of society, not just to the upper echelons. This would likely lead to the creation of some additional social capital—remember the microlenders—as every wage earner gained a reason to pay attention to wealth.

HEALTH CARE

From a risk perspective, the health care system is about to change. Starting in 1998, taxpayers began benefiting from a new tax law that enables them to set aside pretax dollars for medical expenses, just as they put money into an IRA or 401(k). By 2004, the federal budget will have taken an estimated $105 million hit from these medical savings accounts (MSAs).[5] In 1999, MSAs extended to cover Medicare so that individuals can redirect the tax dollars that now go toward Medicare and Medicaid into accounts that would help with future medical expenses. Here's how it works: A twenty-five-year-old making $660 a week sets aside $20 a week, roughly what the IRS now claims for Medicare and Medicaid. If she invests it at 5 percent a year, she'll have a war chest—or, better, a health chest—of more than $152,000 at age seventy-five. Not an answer to everything, but helpful to cover health costs that social insurance programs do not. These investment-oriented accounts could improve the nation's risk position by offsetting real downside risk with financial upside risk. If they catch on, they will likely play the role of charter schools: a thin edge of the wedge that will lead to overall reform.

Like any other significant social change, the coming adjustments in social insurance programs will likely dislocate those least able to participate in and benefit from the risk-taking foundation of future wealth. Societies must prepare for it, even as they shift institutions to accommodate the new aspirations of the citizenry.

LAW AND REGULATION

New public policy to ensure the right risk environment will also mean new laws and regulations. Property rights, for example, are the foundation of a free economy. Since the communists have tried to abolish such rights in Eastern Europe and Asia, and developing nations have struggled to enforce them, surely an economy needs them to prosper as much as it needs bankruptcy law.

According to Bill Sahlman, professor at the Harvard Business School, "The key innovation of the industrial era, much more important than the Bessemer process, steam power, or dozens of other technological inventions, was limited liability, because that's what mobilized capital." Most other countries, both developed and developing, have bankruptcy laws that reflect a past when landed gentry owned the means of production. Then, people loaned money on personal trust, and personal behavior defined risk, not external events such as price movements and natural disasters.

Countries that envy the United States for its entrepreneurial energy and power to innovate should acknowledge the role that risk plays in creating value and adjust their own property and bankruptcy laws accordingly. Risk is the effect of measurable uncertainty in the future, and sometimes that effect is negative. If you make bankruptcy laws too harsh, then the penalty for assuming risk overburdens and discourages entrepreneurs and investors. On the other hand, if risk takers never risk losing because they can lay off their downside risks to their creditors, then they have no incentive to behave prudently.

Just as car insurance may reinforce reckless driving, overly lenient bankruptcy laws encourage fraud or financial imprudence, or what economists call "moral hazard." People take undue risks because they think bankruptcy will rescue them from any downside. In addition, lax bankruptcy laws penalize everyone because lenders seek to recover bankruptcy risks, by raising the interest rates and fees they charge the rest of us or by restricting credit.

The savings and loan industry did just that during the Reagan/Bush years. When elected officials deregulated the thrifts to buy any risk they wanted, they exercised this new freedom feverishly. A few S&L shareholders got very rich, and with very little downside risk. The federal government insured S&L deposits and virtually eliminated the possibility of losses for S&L depositors. But when the investments went sour, the U.S. taxpayer was left with a $481 billion bailout tab.[6]

The S&L crisis was a peculiarly American political phenomenon. The United States not only has relatively more entrepreneurs and more venture capital than any other industrialized nation, it also has the most lenient bankruptcy laws. Chapter 11 of the U.S. Bankruptcy Code gives insolvent companies a degree of protection from their creditors that few other industrialized countries afford.

In one way this demonstrates admirable evolution. Dickensian England hurled debtors into Fleet Prison, hardly the best place for them to earn the money to pay back their creditors. The United States had a better idea and managed the risk differently. It put debtors under protection of the courts to arrange the fairest outcome for borrower and creditor alike. And so Donald Trump went bankrupt, but he remained at large.

This freedom has led to a boom in personal bankruptcy. Despite a thriving economy, a record 1.4 million Americans filed for protection from their creditors in 1998, an increase of nearly 95 percent since 1990.[7] The ease of escaping bankruptcy, and the lack of social stigma at either end of the process, explains part of the phenomenon.

A number of events, including job loss, unexpected health care costs, and lawsuits, can trigger personal bankruptcy. So can overzealous risk taking, or poor business or financial management. Here again, the real question is how to balance freedom and order. Most Americans today, for example, would not repeatedly run up debts gambling at Las Vegas and declare bankruptcy until they hit a lucky streak. Chrysler and Long Term Capital Management, the two U.S. companies bailed out by Congress and the Fed, respectively, weren't gaming the bankruptcy law. But Frank Lorenzo, who declared Continental Airlines bankrupt twice in the eighties to defeat the Machinists Union, probably was.

On the other hand, overly punitive bankruptcy laws could have a chilling effect on risk taking and enterprise. At this writing, the U.S. Congress is considering reform legislation that would restrict individuals with high incomes from filing certain types of bankruptcy and repaying most of their debts. Whatever the outcome, the legislation is designed to restrict abusive bankruptcy filings, without denying access to bankruptcy to those who genuinely need a fresh start. Any society that requires its members to become active risk seekers must protect real risk seekers (entrepreneurs) as well as financial ones (lenders). Policy makers need to have this sort of balanced approach when designing an optimal bankruptcy system.

CREATING THE RIGHT TAX MIX

Taxation is the most powerful tool a government has to redistribute wealth and create incentives for desired behavior.

Current U.S. tax policies focus on income. When the U.S. government instituted the federal income tax in 1913, the tax was levied primarily on a few high-income individuals. The highest tax rate in 1913 was 7 percent, as opposed to 39.6 percent in 1988.[8] New tax policies will shift the focus from income to wealth. Let's look at two possibilities—one from the mainstream and one from the lunatic fringe.

Capital Gains Tax

When it introduced the income tax in 1913, the federal government also started taxing income from capital gains. This capital gains tax, which became one of its more controversial levies in the 1980s, relates directly to risk bearing and future wealth. The capital gains tax taxes the wealthy because it applies to a household's distribution of assets, not its income. As a result, debates tend to polarize, as in "the rich versus the masses." But, as the ordinary U.S.–based investor learned during the stock market "correction" in mid-1998, taxes on wealth increasingly affect all of us. Many mutual funds paid defecting investors share prices that were trading above the levels at which people bought in. These investors incurred capital gains taxes, their first lesson in being "rich." Those who held their shares just about broke even.

Lawmakers want to reduce the capital gains tax to encourage risk bearing, rather than to reward profit taking. Therefore, as wealth derives increasingly from unearned rather than from earned income, governments should develop a tax system that encourages individuals to save and invest rather than consume their wealth. The tax-deductible status of various pension contributions, notably 401(k)s, and a somewhat reduced federal capital gains rate both prompt such investing.

Policy makers might also introduce a broad-based consumption or value-added tax, which theoretically encourages savings and investment over spending because it applies to what goes out, not to what comes in. In 1996, only 17 percent of U.S. tax revenues came from consumption taxes on a handful of goods, such as gasoline and tobacco, while the average for Organization for Economic Cooperation and Development (OECD) countries was almost twice as much.[9]

Finally, the nation might remedy double taxation of corporate income. The current U.S. system taxes corporate dividend income twice: first as net income when the corporation pays its income taxes, and again when the shareholders pay income tax on the dividends they receive. Similarly, U.S. corporations pay payroll taxes, and employees then pay personal income taxes on social security payments. As the share of unearned income increases in the economy, the number of people vexed by such double taxation will increase. Again, the United States is out of synch with its major trading partners, and double taxation adversely effects the ability of U.S. corporations to compete in international capital markets.

Wellness Tax

A progressive health tax could redistribute the financial risk of falling sick. What if it were progressive in both tangible terms— more income, higher tax rate—and intangible—more *health* care, higher tax rate? Currently, individuals carry this financial health risk and lay it off through health insurance. People who change jobs may occasionally lack adequate coverage, and insurers either will not cover or will charge higher premiums for preexisting conditions.

A progressive tax system could tax individuals on the real, intangible asset of their health, not their sickness. In other words, as with the traditional Chinese system, you pay your doctors as long as you remain healthy. If you become sick, then you stop paying and get free medical care until your health returns. This scheme would reflect the truism that without your health, regardless of income, you have nothing.

Just as a progressive income tax hits high-income individuals more, this wellness tax would affect healthy individuals, not sick ones. In other words, it is a progressive wealth tax based on the human capital known as health.

But would a wellness tax discourage healthy living? The proceeds of the progressive income tax suggest not. Think about it: Do you strive to earn less so that you pay less in income taxes? We base this policy suggestion on the same psychology. People are unlikely to want less of what they treasure, wealth or well-being, just because they are taxed according to their financial or physical health.

The tax could be progressive, so that healthy poor people in this scheme wouldn't pay more than sick rich people, or the young, more than the old. Within a given bracket, the healthy pay more. Screening mechanisms would also be necessary, as in insurance and Medicare, not just to discourage those inevitable fakers and crooked doctors, but also to identify and assist those with self-destructive lifestyles—without invading privacy.

Such a policy initiative might actually reduce the risk of falling sick. From an individual's point of view, the policy resembles health insurance, through which the healthy subsidize the sick. Everyone pays premiums, but the sick benefit from treatment, so that their net payment is less. Similarly, under a progressive wellness tax, healthy individuals pay more than ill ones. Uncoupling wellness from costs—indeed, reversing their relationship—opens whole new ways of approaching the health care cost dilemma.

We might view a wellness tax as a mandatory government health insurance program, not so different from Medicare. Converting Medicare, however, from a government defined-benefit health program to a medical savings account with a safety net program would align better with a "risk as opportunity" environment. The government would share in the benefits, namely, what it collects as tax-cum-premiums. Conceivably, companies would also benefit by increased productivity, or they could develop health-based incentive packages: "If you stay healthy so that you're here every day, then we'll pay your health tax." These behavioral interventions could improve the health of the nations, without restricting freedoms of choice.

Changing social insurance, laws and regulations, and tax codes will surely fire up political battles. But all three are vital supporting elements for the financial sector for individuals, business, and society, and must keep pace with major shifts in the economic foundation. The economies that succeed in encouraging risk while dissuading reckless behavior will grow fastest. Higher wires call for stronger nets—and bold, truly innovative regulators and politicians. Vote visionary!

Future Wealth Expectation: *Means tests for taxation, benefits, and scholarships will someday include an evaluation of people's health.*

15

FROM SAFETY TO RISK
Cultural Values for a Connected World

In democracies nothing is more great or more brilliant than commerce: it attracts the attention of the public, and fills the imagination of the multitude: all energetic passions are directed toward it.

[Americans' love of wealth] gives to all their passions a sort of family likeness and soon renders the survey of them exceedingly wearisome.

—ALEXIS DE TOCQUEVILLE
Democracy in America, chapters 17 and 19

MUCH OF THE WORLD outside the United States fears that the American "love of wealth" will cause unwelcome changes in their lives and cultures. The concern is reasonable but untrue. We will have as much economic diversity as we have today, maybe more.

In the newly connected infrastructure, no economy is an island. Future wealth knows no national boundaries. The Internet metaphor of the Web fits our global economy well: There are many routes to every destination. You *can* get to there from here, wherever you are. The smallest change in the most local of infrastructures can have global consequences. Corruption in Russia helps confound the bets of the Long Term Capital Management hedge fund, whose collapse threatens the juggernaut U.S. economy.

The shifts from tangibles to intangibles, from earned to unearned, from saving to investing, from core to derivative, from institution to individual, and from financial measures of the past to those of the future, all rock the world. Globally, people seek income security and wealth accumulation for obvious reasons. If you want to check out your holdings on AOL, then you can choose among the various U.S. exchanges and thirteen other bourses around the world. We trade risk globally with people everywhere. The direction of economic change harmonizes with core American values. The concept of "organizations of one" as an economic enterprise, for example, aligns with the American sense of rugged individualism, from Natty Bumpo of James Fenimore Cooper's classic *Leather-stocking Tales* to Robert Kincaid of Robert James Waller's *The Bridges of Madison County*.

The Marlboro Man embodied this character and has overspread much of the world, at least for the moment. It seems likely that the changes we've described will travel throughout the global economic web as well. We are looking at forces that will affect every part of the connected world. But the forces will play out locally, and uniquely so. The American economy favors flexibility in labor markets, capital markets, and corporate cultures. It lauds open markets and "creative destruction," whereas the Europeans and Japanese mistrust frequent shifts and fear instability. The U.S. approach allows sickly, bloated companies to die and will endure job insecurity, wage stagnation, and growing income inequality.

All of these characteristics make the premise of *Future Wealth* particularly suited to U.S.–based individuals, businesses, infrastructure, and society. Increasingly, American inhabitants recognize that risk is a financial opportunity to embrace and leverage. America's aversion to class structure, though not always practiced, is consistent with financial markets for human capital and will likely flourish in aggressively entrepreneurial economies like those of Israel, Turkey, or the Four Tigers of Asia. All countries—especially those whose citizens invest in markets outside their country's jurisdiction—will strain to balance high-wire incentives with strong, resilient nets.

North Americans value the connectedness of individuals for common purpose, as de Tocqueville observed, but not at the expense of personal freedom. We want our cake, the wickedest of us want to eat it, and we don't want to gain weight either. Wealth without risk, risk without loss, community without oppression, order without control, comprehensive infrastructure but not in one's own backyard. Despite our desires, no value persists without its opposite, the yin/yang of *Future Wealth*. A balanced, healthy tension between them spurs growth, creativity, change, and renewal—all prized values of American business.

APPETITE FOR RISK

Since Queen Isabella played a high-risk hunch in 1492 (crossing vast bodies of water without land in sight), coming to America has meant bearing risk. Every nation resolves the tension between risk and security differently. Capital markets theory says that risk and reward are directly related: Those who bear greater risk receive a greater reward. Nations have chosen their own segment of the risk-return frontier, but one size of risk cannot suit all. If you were an outlier eager for the rewards of higher risk, and your country allowed emigration, you likely headed to the United States. Some

Soviet emigrés who came to America in the 1980s, however, departed, overwhelmed by choice and risk. Most American family trees feature a fortune-seeking ancestor. Perhaps there's a future wealth gene?

Class- or caste-oriented societies inhibit risk bearing, because their members cannot obtain the required resources—financial capital, credibility—to create new value. Those who succeeded against these odds were cast as *arrivistes*. Dare to emigrate, emigrate to risk more, risk more to succeed—that's Horatio Alger's story line.

The connected global economy needs a portfolio of societies bearing different levels and forms of risk, just as your portfolio shouldn't be all cash or all derivatives. When ships were the primary network, access to society operating at a different level of risk required emigration. As the connected economy goes global, you'll be able to trade derivatives almost as easily in the caste-conscious villages of India as in the lofts of Soho. As individuals realize this, they will effectively create a kind of supranational financial system living outside the existing national boundaries. This network exists today, but includes only the likes of Citigroup, Sumitomo, and Soros. Soon, every risk-seeking individual will be playing as well. Collectively, the traffic in risk will have the same effect on national financial systems as do big-time currency speculators: It will put pressure on governments' attempts at isolation.

FINANCIAL SYSTEMS

Many financial innovations have made the capital markets more diverse, accessible, and efficient: venture capital, initial public offerings, electronic communications networks (ECNs), private equity funds. Capitalizing an individual's future earnings seems likely to do the same.

Europe and Japan still lack anything comparable to NASDAQ for incubating ideas and going public. The 500 or so firms in Europe's venture capital community hold some 200,000 companies in their portfolios. Investments of over $30 billion and about a third of venture financing come from commercial banks. But less than 6 percent of Europe's venture money goes to starting new enterprises. Most goes to restructuring existing ownership. Still, innovation is occurring. In Sweden, the government sector constitutes 60 percent of output—almost twice the United States' 32 percent. The Swedish economy combines increasingly aggressive competition, deregulation, and privatization in markets with fully funded health care, guaranteed pensions, and high taxes—essentially a welfare state, a term of pride, not opprobrium, for Sweden. Companies cannot fire full-time workers, but they are hiring more temporary employees. The Swedes have trimmed their national budget deficit to 13 percent of GDP, and their GDP grows at a rate comparable to the United States'.[1] This model seems to combine the best of high levels of business risk with low personal risk, and it bears watching. Assuming it succeeds, might it work in the United States? Americans might not want security at the price of a more equal income distribution. But if the have/have-nots issue becomes more pressing, they just might.

In Japan, the deeply rooted conservatism at the highest levels of business leadership and the devastating mismatch between eager investors and capital-hungry companies impede progress. Its over-the-counter market serves small, well-established companies in traditional industries, not risky entrepreneurial ventures.

The coziness of large enterprises and their bankers helped to precipitate the recent Japanese recession. In 1988, the Nikkei Index, as a measure of the value of the Japanese stock market, was at 30,000. The Dow Jones Industrial Index was at 2,500. Of the ten biggest banks worldwide, nine were Japanese.[2] Relationships counted more than performance. Cronyism influenced stock market valuation and bank asset allocation and procedures, as well as formal and informal practices of lending, accounting, and bankruptcy. What would lose face in Japan would earn a red badge of courage in Silicon Valley.

Ten years later, the Nikkei had lost 70 percent of its value, while the Dow Jones had gained 250 percent. The world's ten largest banks only include one Japanese institution formed in 1998 by the merger of Tokyo and Mitsubishi banks.[3] Over the last ten years, the international yardstick of the global financial sector has replaced Japanese metrics. The growing interconnectedness of the financial sector has pressured banks to restructure their business practices along international standards.

By those measures, Japanese bank loans are bad loans, because the banks based decisions on poor accounting methods, insufficient collateral value, and insufficient recourse for lenders—today this serves as an instructive example of reckless, high-risk investment—"collateralized" by little more than trust in relationships and the Japanese economy.

Adopting the standard of the global financial sector hurts: It shifts the Darwinian rules for the accumulation, control, and distribution of wealth. It forces unhealthy banks and companies into bankruptcy and causes short-term losses for investors. Japan has struggled with this survival of the fittest for years, en route to more efficient capital markets. Malaysia successfully but temporarily unplugged its economy from the connected marketplace by installing capital flow restrictions and other crisis mismanagement ploys. But in the long run, national leaders have only two sustainable choices: efficient markets or isolation from the connected economy.

During bearish times, Americans tend to long for Japanese and European models. Stability, quality of life, long-term security, lifetime employment all seem the antidote to what ails the U.S. and global economies. The more entrepreneurial they try to be, the less comfortably they fit. Meanwhile, during periods of rapid technological change and bullish economic growth, Americans praise flexibility and risk taking. The efficient market view says that inherent systemic suppleness can endure seismic shifts in economic infrastructure.

The invisible hand of innate creativity will exploit upside potential in a new economy.

SOCIAL SYSTEMS

The increased life expectancy in industrialized countries has pressured many non–U.S. economies to address their pensions, social security, unemployment benefits, and health care programs. The postwar United States lagged behind Western Europe in creating social systems to bear risks for individuals—national health programs, laws restricting job elimination, protective tariffs. Recently, countries like the United Kingdom and Sweden have recognized that their public or social institutions can no longer guarantee the benefits nor absorb the risks of these programs. Virtually all industrialized countries must reassess the extent to which they will shift responsibility to the individual.

As we move from the early to the later half of the information age, the connected economy will necessitate development of safety nets to protect individuals from catastrophic loss without eliminating individual accountability. The United States may lead now in capitalizing on the shift from crunching to connecting, but even the poorest risk-oriented economies have a real opportunity to pioneer whole solutions and set international standards. In between, as noted, Sweden is pioneering a third way.

CULTURE CONVERGENCE

Technology hastens to connect us globally, and not exclusively in financial markets. Volatility and unpredictability, enormous and rapid swings, and financial hiccups in one corner of the globe hit all corners of the world with political and cultural ramifications. How can we thrive in this intense connectedness, while politely maintaining our cultural distinctions?

Many countries understandably welcome America's economic values more than its cultural ones. Many fear that adopting the latter includes such American social problems as higher rates of violent crime and teenage pregnancy.

Lee Kwan Yew, modern history's most successful benevolent dictator, scoffs at American reactions to Singapore's sometimes draconian law, pointing to the combination of stunning economic growth and a highly civil society. Singapore already ranks among the most connected nations, pioneering in the 1980s, for example, the electronic delivery of government services.

How connectedness influences the economic development of different countries will vary, but all will of necessity devise business practices compatible with the connected economy, like electrical adapters that allow travelers to plug in to a foreign power network. This is what Tony Blair's policy consultant, Geoff Mulgan, calls "connexity."[4] That the U.S. has an early lead in connecting does not mean all others will follow the same path, any more than it meant all industrializing countries followed England's exact path.

The global economic powers can learn from each other. America embraces risk-taking individualism, Japan values the close-knitted social fabric, and Europe offers social safety nets. How the global connected economy develops in any one region or country will surely reflect local cultural characteristics. Future wealth will benefit from such an ecology of value systems, always cross-breeding with each other.

Walk the streets in any world-class city and watch your fellow pedestrians touch microphones dangling near their chins to accept a phone call, wherever they are, whatever they're doing. The Finnish cell phone leader Nokia has even developed a way to call a Coke machine so that thirsty customers can drink without coins.[5] The next wave of innovation will come from every place that embraces connectedness—Shanghai and Stockholm, as well as Silicon Valley. As net access goes global, the computer-literate generation, more globally minded than ever before, will likely craft the next set of social adaptations. The Internet both enables and blazes trails, because connectivity, market efficiency, and risk are so tightly linked.

A breathtaking example is the Junior Summit, sponsored by Sega, Swatch, and Citigroup, organized by MIT's Media Lab, and led by Professor Justine Cassell. MIT solicited ideas globally from children ten to sixteen, asking how technology could be used to make a better world. The invitations were sent by every means— through embassies, school systems, and, of course, the Net. MIT then created a connected community among the 1,000 children selected from 15,000 responses. Steps were taken to provide Internet connectivity for all 1,000 (including Professor Cassell bringing computers to the children in Africa). The children debated their ideas for a year, ultimately selecting 100 from among themselves to attend a week-long summit in November 1988 at MIT. There, they narrowed down their suggestions to just six. And a year later, the group is organizing Kidzbank, "to be run and managed by kids. This bank will fund projects aimed at improving the lives of underprivileged children around the world."[6] It is designed to raise its capital from both concerned consumers and companies interested in marketing to kids. Kidzbank is an adapter—a global approach to plugging into the financial economy. Communication, capital, and risk are inseparable.

The adoption of the Net and other recent connecting technologies foreshadows how future wealth may spread. With breathtaking speed, the Net is providing the world's population with access to ideas and opportunity. Radio Free Europe, fax machines in China, and televisions in the Middle East have all freed the flow of information to spread notions about freedom and autonomy. With such potent ideas, subtly but inevitably, come those of risk and individual accountability.

As many Internet proponents (freedom fighters) before us have noted, the Net supports diversity of opinion like no medium before it. Broadcasting is a one-way conversation, and telephones reach only a few people at a time. The Net allows any subject, viewpoint, person to exist in the global ideaspace. American, Singaporean, and Slav teens can and do debate the merits of their respective cultures and economic systems every day, separately and together. This process engenders convergence on some issues, divergence on others, and heightened awareness overall. It will not, however, produce cultural hegemony, because future wealth—efficient markets for human capital and risk—thrives on both diversity and individuality, and no one person or power can control its forces. We can even hope for this conversation to nourish social capital, in the form of increased understanding of and respect for cultural and individual differences around the world.

Now that would be lasting future wealth.

Future Wealth Expectation: *One of the first broad commercial uses of low earth orbital satellites will be to establish creditworthiness anyplace on the globe.*

PART V

horizons

CONNECTIVITY leads to commerce, commerce to wealth, wealth to risk, risk to risk trading. This is true for individuals, enterprise, and society. It's what future wealth is about. There's no magic solution to this world, but there *are* new guidelines. Try the twenty that follow, and let us know which ones make sense, which don't, and the ones you think we left out.

TWENTY PERFECT FUTURES

New software, more powerful computers, cheaper telephone service, regulatory changes, the advent of low-cost on-line brokerage services— the earthquake these forces have set off in the American marketplace is far from over.[1]

BY NOW YOU KNOW that *Future Wealth* isn't a get-rich-quick book. No "Five Easy Steps to Your First Billion" here. It is more a perspective on the profound changes that are sweeping over the global economy. Only by recognizing change can you embrace it, and only by welcoming it can you survive and prosper in the years ahead.

Here are twenty ways toward future wealth which we think count the most. The heavy lifting is up to you.

1. CONNECT AND PARTICIPATE

Sometimes the economic landscape's tectonic plates shift profoundly, upending the status quo and reversing bodies in motion. Because the Internet changes life as we know it, the big play in the information economy has shifted from crunching to connecting. The financial dimension of the economy ascends as the real dimension recedes. Recognize the signs: You face great change, unprecedented risk, and ever more opportunity.

2. FOCUS ON NET WORTH, NOT INCOME

A salary by itself never made anyone wealthy. Consider it walking-around money and concentrate instead on the whole asset portfolio. The source of future wealth is shifting from earned money to money that works for you—from earned to unearned. Rename your nest egg your "invest egg." 401(k)s and IRAs yield future wealth.

3. MAKE FINANCIAL RISK WORK FOR YOU

The greater the risk, the greater the rewards. Insuring our homes, headquarters, and other tangible property reduces downside risk. Insuring or otherwise safeguarding our human and financial assets—buying Treasury bills rather than Internet stocks, or opting for high salary–low equity compensation over low salary–high equity mix—caps the upside risk as well as the possible return. Downside risk protection limits potential losses; it sets the floor. Upside risk protection limits prospective opportunities; it sets the ceiling rather than creates a skylight. Be risk's taskmaster, not its slave.

4. BUILD FINANCIAL MARKETS FOR HUMAN CAPITAL

Financial markets already provide investors with a place for betting on the future performance of corporations through stocks and bonds.

We now need to build comparable markets for packaging and trading human capital. The architects and erectors of this new securities industry stand to reap huge rewards in the coming millennium. The operatives and the asset-rich also stand to gain by preparing themselves to trade both others' and their own human capital, starting by posting résumés and surfing the Internet for talent.

5. RAISE THE WIRES (EVEN HIGHER) AND STRENGTHEN THE NETS

Societies that want to create future wealth must encourage risk taking by weaving more durable safety nets that simultaneously are broader and more selective. They are society's equivalent of insuring against downside financial risk. Citizens (of democracies) should insist that their local, regional, and national representatives and legislators reexamine social insurance (social security, health care, retirement insurance), personal bankruptcy, and taxation.

INDIVIDUALS

6. TREAT YOUR LABOR AS A TRADABLE SECURITY

All individuals have future earnings potential, and the more intellectual capital that each person controls, the greater the personal potential is. Like song writers and other artists and athletes, high-end professionals with bankable intellectual capital will eventually securitize their long-range income (earned and unearned) just as companies now raise capital by selling stock and bonds. Within two decades, this market will have experienced accelerated growth, volatility, abuse, regulation, innovation, globalization, and, ultimately, respectability. Retiring baby boomers will miss some of this direct opportunity but can advise and invest in up-and-coming Gen-X'ers.

7. PREPARE FOR WEALTH

Control of wealth has migrated from feudal lords, robber barons, corporate managers, and pension funds to individuals. Employee loyalty no longer guarantees job security, and the benefits department no longer decides where to invest employee retirement funds. Instead of one-size-fits-all pension plans, workers can now pick their own mix of risks and returns for their retirement portfolios. Employees should secure their own human capital, not their job.

8. TRUST THE MARKET TO DETERMINE REWARDS

As workers take control of their financial futures, more of them by changing jobs or starting companies, they begin to realize and accept that they really work for themselves regardless of the formal contract. Market forces, as much as their elbow grease and brainpower, influence economic outcomes. Individuals must now focus on a more direct relationship between effort and equity, wages and wealth, income and investments.

9. MANAGE THE ASSET ALREADY AT RISK

Most of us trade risk all the time, whether negotiating work compensations, benefits packages, or accepting jobs. Do we pay a high premium for maximum medical coverage or bet that no one will get sick? Do we buy and sell stocks, bonds, or both? Assemble an integrated picture of all your risks, upside and downside, in your control and beyond, and learn to manage them as an entirety. If you can measure the risk, then you can eventually package and trade it.

10. CREATE WHILE YOU TRADE

As people begin acting like investments, they must operate to grow, not to settle or collect. Those who trade assets produce nothing of value even if their portfolios grow. Those who produce value create wealth in society.

COMPANIES

11. DEVELOP STRATEGIC RISK UNITS (SRUs) TO OPTIMIZE THE VALUE OF RISKS IN BUSINESS

Companies must analyze their risks to determine not only which to take, but also how best to manage and trade to the highest bidder. For example, should a company buy its key supplier or hedge against the loss of supply? Strategic risk units (SRUs) can measure and trade the risks that go with such situations. As equal partners of strategic business units (SBUs), they can help companies to trade risk actively. As such, they'd leverage core value and discover new value that may cut across SBUs and the entire company. Risk presents opportunity as well as trouble. Companies should seek out and optimize it.

12. RUN THE ORGANIZATION BY MARKETPLACE RULES

Most organizations change far more slowly than their competitive environments, because their leaders run them by internal rules of politics, status, and psychology rather than by laws of economics. Internal rules change arithmetically, whereas external realities change exponentially. How can you train your organization to keep up? Externalize it. Outsourcing and organizing can virtually move a firm in this direction, but managers must give most if not all employees direct contact with external forces and eliminate departments that serve only the internal customers. A new generation of data mining and management tools, as well as communications devices and infrastructure, will create the as yet oxymoronic real-time organization—as fast to change as the market it serves.

13. MANAGE HUMAN RESOURCES AS AN ASSET

To the future wealthy, people are assets, literally and not metaphorically or pejoratively. Only when companies position human resources as an assets function instead of an administrative one, and only when they mark these assets regularly to market will they develop the full value of this intellectual capital. Only then will CEOs treat their head of human resources as the equal of their chief financial officer.

14. INVEST IN EMPLOYEES—LITERALLY

Investing in the human capital of employees benefits both workers and owners. Employees get financial rewards now for future performance and reduced downside risk in exchange for a portion of their upside. Companies get a tradable piece of employees' future earnings, regardless of employer, occupation, or term of employees' revenues. But first a company must unbundle its intangible intellectual assets—the workers on its payroll, its patents, its customer relationships, its copyrights—from its tangible assets, such as factories and machinery. Then it must devise employment agreements that—like contracts between authors and publishers—outlast the period of actual employment. First, unbundle. Next, package. Then, invest. Finally, trade.

15. LIVE IN CONNECTED ECONOMY TIME

Seek value in the future, not the past, and in the continuum, not the period. Using the past to measure value works well with wines, but not with wineries. Value companies as venture capitalists do, by their growth potential, not by growth achieved. Assets tell you where a company has been; income, where a company is; market capitalization, where a company is headed; and risk, at what rate of acceleration. A company overflowing with tangible assets may be too heavy to run the race. Grow your intangible:tangible (*i:t*) ratio faster than your competition does and you'll win. Live in the 24-by-7 world. Measure and adjust asset flows continuously instead of periodically. Close your books monthly, then weekly, and as soon as possible continuously. Adjust your prices, products, services, and salaries; your projects, processes, and policies; and your roster and risks relentlessly. Then brace yourself for future wealth.

SOCIETY

16. ADVOCATE CAPITAL MARKETS AS THE NEW EMANCIPATORS

In the industrial age, workers used political means such as socialism and trade unions for economic gain. In the first half of the Information Age, worker-controlled retirement plans like IRAs and 401(k)s bestow greater economic equality. In the second half, the once-despised capital markets may emancipate the masses, as Karl Marx stirs in his London grave. True, such economic mechanisms create equity, not equality, as political or philosophical methods might. But to the extent that capital markets help individuals maximize the financial potential of their intellect and talent, they also advance a more meritocratic society.

17. WEALTH IS NO LONGER JUST FOR THE WEALTHY

In 1999, stocks accounted for 20 percent of all U.S. household financial assets, a dramatic increase from 1990's 12 percent.[2] The bottom line: Middle-class wealth is no oxymoron. This reorientation of wealth is benefiting the very poor through, for example, microlending programs in Bangladesh, South Africa, and impoverished areas of the United States. A low-end personal computer, an Internet connection, a sound business idea, and a solid education can unleash the wealth of the global marketplace. The super rich are irrelevant. Future wealth means no entitlements, just opportunities.

18. VOTE FOR A NEW TAX SYSTEM

The tax man's role will change when society implements new laws to encourage prudent risk taking and to provide safety nets. He might impose consumption taxes instead of income taxes, to encourage wealth building, or other tax-free vehicles for saving and investing. Regardless, he will likely aim new codes at the biggest driver of new wealth—human capital, as well as other intangibles. After all, he switched from land to the products of factories after the last infrastructure shift.

19. LOBBY FOR GLOBAL DIVERSITY, MARKET EFFICIENCY, FLEXIBILITY, AND CULTURAL TOLERANCE

The global marketplace and the global ubiquity of the Internet have rendered obsolete or antiquated totally isolated economies. Future wealth flourishes in America's cultural preferences for flexibility in labor markets, capital markets, and corporate cultures; for open markets, individualism, and level playing fields. U.S.–based professionals enjoy venture capital markets far more evolved than those in Europe and Japan. Countries and international conglomerates can fine-tune these notions of future wealth to accommodate their national cultures and ignore the rest. We hope that our Web site and business propositions help all readers of *Future Wealth* to understand how they might improve and implement our ideas in economies around the world.

20. BEWARE OF WHAT YOU WANT–
WEALTH IS FOR BETTER AND FOR WORSE

No society can survive utter self-absorption. Money can liberate or enslave us, stimulate or suffocate us. Money alone is sterile. Only productive assets procreate or propagate hearty value. Will a rush to wealth creation crush that simple economic proposition? Will day trading replace caring? Will profit taking replace philanthropy? Possibly. We're not Pollyannas. Every economic transition of the past has caused problems, like the sweatshops and slums of the industrial revolution. Ultimately, most of these maladies—though certainly not all—were cured. Use wealth to breed greed, and we're all diseased. Use wealth as a form of fitness to emancipate individuals, and world society takes another giant step forward.

Notes

CHAPTER 1 FROM INCOME TO WEALTH

1. Jeff Donn, "6 Percent Are Web Addicts," *Associated Press Online*, 23 August 1999.

2. U.S. Department of Commerce, *Statistical Abstract of the United States: 1975* (Washington, D.C.: Government Printing Office, 1975); U.S. Department of Commerce, *Statistical Abstract of the United States: 1977* (Washington, D.C.: Government Printing Office, 1977); *Economic Report of the President* (Washington, D.C.: Government Printing Office, 1975, 1991, 1999).

3. S&P Market Insight, Industry Report: Computers "Hardware." (S&P data from IDC) and S&P Market Insight Industry Report; Industry Name: Computers (Software & Services) Computers: Commercial Services Industry Survey, July 1999.

4. Louis Uchitelle, "Greenspan Ties Debate on Rates to the Markets," *New York Times*, 28 August 1999. Copyright © 1999 by the New York Times Co. Reprinted by permission.

5. Authors' calculation, from data from OneSource Global Business Browser, 9 November 1999, <http://globalbb.onesource.com>, using data provided by Market Guide, Info. US and Corp. Tech.

6. Internal Revenue Service, <97inprel.exe at http://www.irs.gov/tax_stats/soi/soi_bul.html>. The statistical increase understates the importance of income from investments, because it does not include unrealized capital gains from tax-deferred retirement assets.

7. Investment Company Institute, *Mutual Funds Factbook* 1999 (Washington, D.C.: Investment Company Institute, 1999). Also available at <www.ici.org/aboutfunds/factbook_toc.html>.

8. "Worker Capitalist," *Wall Street Journal*, 30 November 1999.

CHAPTER 2   FROM EARLY TO LATE INFORMATION AGE

1. John Sculley with John A. Byrne, *Odyssey: Pepsi to Apple—A Journey of Adventure, Ideas, and the Future* (New York: Harper & Row, 1987).

2. "About E*Trade," <http://etrade.com>.

3. Thomas K. Grose, "Virtual Bourses," *Time International*, 4 October 1999, 62.

4. Amy Harmon, "Auction for a Kidney Pops Up on Ebay's Site," *New York Times*, 3 September 1999.

5. Christopher Meyer, personal conversation at the National Computer Board, Singapore, circa 1993.

6. This is the thesis of Francis Fukuyama's *The Great Disruption: Human Nature and the Reconstitution of Social Order* (New York: Free Press, 1999), in which Fukuyama argues that every economic revolution produces a social counterpart.

7. Insurance company example: Reuters, "Progressive Tests Tracking System for Car Insurance," 25 October 1999, <http://business.yahoo.com/rf/991025/2c.html>. Divorce example: Don Feder, "Seductive Cyberspace Sinks Marriage," *Boston Herald*, 5 July 1999.

CHAPTER 3   FROM BARTER TO BLOOMBERG

1. CAPM rests on some important assumptions that cannot be empirically verified—for example, that variations in return are

normally distributed. For several reasons, finance theorists are reevaluating CAPM. Nonetheless, it has established universally the idea of trade-offs between the expected volatility of an investment—a definition of its riskiness—and its expected return. See Peter L. Bernstein, *Against the Gods: The Remarkable Story of Risk* (New York: John Wiley & Sons, 1996).

2. Robert E. Rubin, "Remarks before the World Economic Conference, Davos, Switzerland" (speech given at the World Economic Forum, Davos, Switzerland, 30 January 1999).

3. Some people prefer a broader definition of probability that includes subjective indices.

4. Bernstein, *Against the Gods,* 337.

5. Peter Henig, "Experts Agree: Zero Margins Won't Work," 18 May 1999, <http://www.redherring.com/insider/1999/0518/inv-zero margins.html> (20 August 1999).

6. Daniel Eisenberg, "We're for Hire, Just Click," *Time*, 16 August 1999, 46.

7. Jeffrey Taylor, CEO of Monster.com, interview by Christopher Meyer and Christoph Knoess, Cambridge, Mass., 9 June 1999.

8. Anne Tergesen, "Private Equity for the Hoi Polloi? Not Quite, but You Don't Need to Be Superrich to Buy In," *Business Week*, 16 August 1999, 118.

CHAPTER 4   FROM PAYCHECK TO PORTFOLIO

1. "Sammy Sosa Slams Michael Jordan in Restaurant Switch," *South China Morning Post*, 25 September 1999. Reprinted by permission of the Associated Press.

2. Neal Stephenson, *The Diamond Age, or, a Young Lady's Illustrated Primer* (New York: Bantam Books, 1995).

3. Mark Borden and Suzanne Koudsi, "America's Forty Richest Under Forty," *Fortune*, 27 September 1999, 89.

4. Jerry Useem and Wilton Woods, "For Sale Online: You," *Fortune*, 5 July 1999, 66.

CHAPTER 5   FROM CORPORATE COG TO MARKET CAP

1. Andrew Postman, "I'm Taking My Family Public," *New York Times*, 9 July 1999. Copyright © 1999 by the New York Times Co. Reprinted by permission.

2. "The Man Who Sold the Bond: David Bowie Issues $55 Million Worth of Ten-Year Bonds Backed by His Hits," 6 February 1997, <http://www.cnnfn.com/hotstories/bizbuzz/9702/07/bowiesbonds.pkg/>.

3. Robert Sablowsky, David Pullman, and William Zysblatt, separate interviews with Nikolas Kron, Cambridge, Mass., October 1999.

4. Ibid.

5. Ibid.

6. Antony Currie, "Borrowers: Is This the Biggest Show in Town?" <http://www.geocities.com/WallStreet/Exchange/1574/secure showbizz.htm> (June 1998).

7. Ibid.

8. Authors' calculation, using data from Hollywood Stock Exchange, 7 July 1999, <http://www.hsx.com>.

9. See <http://services.golfweb.com/ga/bios/spga/trevino_lee.html>.

10. Stan Davis, personal conversation with Dutch colleagues.

11. "The Man Who Sold the Bond."

12. William Krasilovsky, "From Rock 'N Roll to Respectability: Securitizing Music Royalties" (presentation at forum on Music and Motion Picture Revenues & Royalties Securitization, Windows on the World, New York, 7 May 1998).

13. Ibid.

14. David Pullman, president and CEO of the Pullman Group, telephone interview with Nikolas Kron, Cambridge, Mass., October 1999.

CHAPTER 6   FROM WORKER TO PLAYER

1. DOONESBURY © 1999, G.B. Trudeau. Reprinted with permission of UNIVERSAL PRESS SYNDICATE. All rights reserved.

2. Authors' calculation, using data from Hollywood Stock Exchange, 15 June 1999, <http://www.hsx.com>.

3. Stephen M. Pollan and Mark Levine, *Live Rich: Everything You Need to Know to Be Your Own Boss, Whoever You Work For* (New York: HarperBusiness, 1998).

4. Ibid.

5. Reprinted by permission of Felix Cavaliere.

CHAPTER 7   FROM RISK AS PROBLEM TO RISK AS OPPORTUNITY

1. Arthur B. Kennickell, Martha Starr-McCleur, and Annika E. Sunden, "Family Finances in the U.S.: Recent Evidence from the Survey of Consumer Finances," *Federal Reserve Bulletin*, January 1997.

2. For a copy of the report, see <http://www.nfow.com/nforesearch/nfoi_brokerage.asp>.

CHAPTER 8   FROM SBUS TO SRUS

1. See Diane Brady, "Insurance: Is Your Bottom Line Covered?" *Business Week*, 8 February 1999; and "Insurer Tunes Up Music Plagiarism Policy . . ." *Wall Street Journal*, 26 January 1999.

2. James P. Miller, "Buffett Again Declines to Flinch at Stock Market's High-Wire Act," *Wall Street Journal*, 5 May 1998.

3. "Can Insurers Offer Coverage for Earnings?" *Wall Street Journal*, 29 December 1998. Also available at <http://www.timesmirror.com/companies/>.

4. "Reducing Risk Doesn't Pay Off," *Wall Street Journal*, 15 March 1999.

5. Marcia Vickers, "Are Two Stocks Better Than One?" *Business Week*, 28 June 1999.

6. See <http://www.investaweather.com/media/savemills.html>.

7. Mark Golden and Ed Silliere, "Report on Business: Can't Fool Mother Nature?" 13 March 1999, <http://www.investaweather.com/media/savemills.htm> (27 October 1999).

8. "Ancor's Warrants Deal with Sun Microsystems Is Sweet for Customer, Less So for Switch Firm," *Wall Street Journal*, 10 September 1999.

CHAPTER 9   FROM INSIDE TO OUTSIDE

1. Robert Lenzner and Stephen S. Johnson, "Seeing Things as They Really Are," 10 March 1997, <http://www.forbes.com/forbes/97/0310/5905122a.htm> (11 November 1999).

2. Larry Downes and Chunka Mui, *Unleashing the Killer App: Digital Strategies for Market Dominance* (Boston: Harvard Business School Press, 1998).

3. Jeffrey Taylor, CEO of Monster.com, telephone interview with Christopher Meyer and Christoph Knoess, Cambridge, Mass., 9 June 1999.

4. John Kao, *Jamming: The Art and Discipline of Business Creativity* (New York: HarperBusiness, 1997).

CHAPTER 10   FROM PAYROLLS TO PORTFOLIOS

1. Director of Great People was chosen as one of *Fast Company*'s job titles of the future. We think the idea, not the title, will succeed. Shannon Spring, "Job Titles of the Future: Barb Karlin," Fast Company, February 1999, 46.

2. Richard A. Melcher with Carol Matlack, "Manpower: 'I'm Working My Tail Off to Fix the Company,'" *Business Week*, 16 August 1999.

3. Jeffrey Taylor, CEO of Monster.com, interview by Christopher Meyer and Christoph Knoess, Cambridge, Mass., 9 June 1999.

4. Jerry Useem and Wilton Woods, "For Sale Online: You," *Fortune*, 5 July 1999, 66.

5. Ibid.

6. Ibid.

7. "Diamondbacks Strike Again, Sign Johnson to 4-Year Deal. $52 Million Keeps Pitcher Close to Home," *Orlando Sentinel*, 1 December 1998.

8. John A. Byrne, "For Top Talent, How Green Is the Valley: E-Commerce Sparks a Bidding War for CEOs," *Business Week*, 9 August 1999.

CHAPTER 11   FROM VESTING TO INVESTING

1. Abby Ellin, "Business Schools Are Investing in Their Student Entrepreneurs: Venture Funds Provide Powerful Show of Faith," *The San Diego Union-Tribune*, 7 August 1999.

2. James J. Mitchell, "What the Boss Makes: Anxiety Rises over Stock Options in a Bear Market," *KRTBN Knight-Ridder*

Tribune Business News: San Jose Mercury News—California, 13 June 1999.

3. Ibid.

4. From Stan Davis' notes on Greg Maffei's presentation at Forbes' CFO Conference, Charleston, S.C., 5 May 1999.

5. "Riding the Storm," *The Economist*, 6 November 1999, 63–64.

CHAPTER 12 FROM PAST TO FUTURE

1. "Measures That Matter," Ernst & Young Center for Business Innovation White Paper, Cambridge, Mass., September 1999; Jonathan Low and Tony Siesfeld, "Measures That Matter: Wall Street Considers Non-Financial Performance More Than You Think," *Strategy & Leadership* 26, no. 2 (March/April 1998): 24.

2. Darr Beiser, "Cisco Chief Pushes 'Virtual Close,'" *USA Today Tech*, 12 October 1999.

CHAPTER 13 FROM MARX TO MARKETS

1. Board of Governors of the Federal Reserve System, *Flow of Funds Accounts of the United States Flows and Outstandings Second Quarter: 1999* (Washington, D.C.: Government Printing Office, 1999); Board of Governors of the Federal Reserve System, *Flow of Funds Coded Tables 20 September, 1994* (Washington, D.C.: Government Printing Office, 1994).

2. "Investors, Unite," from *A Survey of Fund Management*, 25 October 1997, 3. © 1997 The Economist Newspaper Group, Inc. Reprinted with permission. Further reproduction prohibited. <www.economist.com>.

3. U.S. Bureau of the Census, *Measuring 50 Years of Economic Change Using the March Current Population Survey*, Current Population Reports, P60-203 (Washington, D.C.: Government Printing Office, 1998), C20.

4. Robert Lenzner and Stephen S. Johnson, "Seeing Things as They Really Are," 10 March 1997, <http://www.forbes.com/forbes/97/0310/5905122a.htm> (11 November 1999).

5. Kevin Kelly, "Wealth Is Overrated," *Wired* 6.03, March 1998. © 1998 The Condé Nast Publications Inc. All rights reserved. Reprinted by permission.

6. Bill Gates, with Nathan Myhrvold and Peter Rinearson, *The Road Ahead* (New York: Viking, 1995), 58.

7. Roxana Frost (speech presented at Ernst & Young's Measuring the Future Conference, Cambridge, Mass., 27 October 1999).

8. Katie Hafner, "Common Ground Elusive as Technology Have-Nots Meet Haves," *New York Times*, 8 July 1999.

9. John Stackhouse, "Village Phones Ring Up Profit: CELL-PHONE CRAZE," *The Globe and Mail*, 6 July 1998.

10. Tom Neubig, Gautam Jaggi, and Robin Lee, *Chapter 7 Bankruptcy Petitioners' Repayment Ability Under H.R. 833: The National Perspective* (Washington, D.C.: Ernst & Young LLP, 1999). Also available at <http://www.ey.com/publicate/eyecon/pdf/report99.pdf> (November 1, 1999).

11. Stackhouse, "Village Phones Ring Up Profit."

12. "A Look at the Balance Sheet," <http://www.grameen-info.org/bank/lookbs.html> (11 November 1999).

13. United Nations Economic Commission for Africa, *Economic Report on Africa 1999: The Challenges of Poverty Reduction and Sustainability*, United Nations, <http://www.un.org/Depts/eca/divis/espd/ecrep99.htm> (9 September 1999).

CHAPTER 14   FROM DEBTORS' PRISON TO CHAPTER 11

1. Social Security Administration, *1999 Annual Report of the Board of Trustees of The Federal Old-Age and Survivors Insurance and Disability Insurance Trust Funds*, March 1999; "Plenty for Social Security," *Washington Post*, 24 November 1998.

2. Martin Feldstein, "America's Golden Opportunity," *The Economist*, 13 March 1999, 41.

3. José Piñera, "Empowering People," testimony before the U.S. Senate Committee on Banking, Housing and Urban Affairs Subcommittee on Securities, 26 June 1997. Available at <http://www.pensionreform.org/articles/ct-jp062597.html> (11 November 1999).

4. Feldstein, "America's Golden Opportunity."

5. *Budget of the United States Government: Analytical Perspectives Fiscal Year 2000* (Washington, D.C. Government Printing Office), 1999.

6. Rob Wells, "S&L Bailout Cost $481 Billion, Up from Previous Estimates," *The Detroit News*, 13 July 1996.

7. Administrative Office of the U.S. Courts, *Increase in Bankruptcy Filings Slows in Fiscal Year 1998* (Washington, D.C.: Government Printing Office, 1998).

8. Joseph A. Pechman, *Federal Tax Policy* (Washington, D.C.: Brookings Institution, 1987), 63, 313; Peter W. Bernstein, ed., *The Ernst & Young Tax Guide 1998* (New York: John Wiley & Sons, 1998).

9. "Taxation, 1996,"<http://www.oecd.org/publications/figures/e_38-39_taxation.pdf> (10 November 1999).

CHAPTER 15   FROM SAFETY TO RISK

1. Edmund L. Andrews, "Sweden, the Welfare State, Basks in a New Prosperity," *New York Times*, 8 October 1999.

2. "The Business of Banking," *The Economist*, October 30–November 5, 1999, 89–90.

3. Ibid.

4. Geoff Mulgan, *Connexity: How to Live in a Connected World* (Boston: Harvard Business School Press, 1998).

5. Charles P. Wallace, "Psion of the Times," *Time International*, 23 November 1998.

6. From the Kidzbank charter; see <http://www.jrsummit.net/tpls/why_jrs.wpi?pageID=992701140109EN&dd>.

CHAPTER 16   TWENTY PERFECT FUTURES

1. Diana Henriques, *The New York Times Book Review*, 14 November 1999, 32.

2. Board of Governors of the Federal Reserve System, *Flow of Funds Accounts of the United States Flows and Outstandings Second Quarter: 1999* (Washington, D.C.: Government Printing Office, 1999); Board of Governors of the Federal Reserve System, *Flow of Funds Coded Tables 20 September, 1994* (Washington, D.C.: Government Printing Office, 1994).

Acknowledgments

The intellectual assets of *Future Wealth*, whatever their merits, represent the investment of many people's human capital. First among them is Nikolas Kron, whose ability to control two authors, in the same place all too seldom, was both essential and uncanny. Without him, *Future Wealth* would never have been created, accumulated, nor distributed.

Jeff Greene, leader of Ernst & Young's Capital Markets practice, provided essential support—intellectual, moral, and financial. Our colleagues at Ernst & Young—Terry Ozan, Rick Bobrow, Bill Lipton, Doug Phillips, Bill Arnone, and Phil Lawrence—also came to the aid of the project. Perry Quick, Tom Neubig, and Steve Tanny in particular devoted time to reviewing our drafts.

Our partners in writing and editing, Colin Leinster and Howard Means, contributed their ears and pens to help structure and texture the manuscript. If you've understood *Future Wealth*, to a large degree we have them to thank.

Gautam Jaggi and Christoph Knoess added essential insights, data, and examples to our work, assisted by Ashilan Dolen and Roderick Hall. Virtually all of the staff of the Ernst & Young Center for Business Innovation deserve our gratitude for critiquing early drafts and becoming part of a scouting network, providing daily examples from their own research that might help the book. Jennifer Cline, Megan O'Rourke, Jill Therrien, and Laura Senior McGoff converted the invisible and indecipherable into a clean manuscript again and again with inexplicable good humor. Our agent and advocate, Rafe Sagalyn, recognized that Harvard Business School Press was the right house for our ideas. Our editor, Kirsten Sandberg, showed enthusiasm, dedication, and determination from start to finish. She was resolute about winning the competition to publish *Future Wealth* and she was always there with time, energy, knowledge, talent, and heart, helping us to shape our vision. HBS Press executives Carol Franco and Gayle Treadwell also believed deeply in the project and supported us throughout.

There have been many helpful conversations with knowledgeable people in the risk and human capital industries. James K. Cornell, Christopher de Rahm, David Dryer, Joel Friedman, Kevin Kelly, David Pullman, Andy Rapaport, Mary Rivet, Steve Resnick, Jonathan Schwartz, Jeff Taylor, George Vojta, and Walt Wriston have been informative, critical, and stimulating.

Index

ABB, 98

accountability, 33, 155, 157

accounting practices, 61, 86, 108–109, 111, 115, 116, 153, 167

Adams, John, 22

Adidas, 48

Africa, 133, 134, 157, 167

Against the Gods (Bernstein), 28

Amazon.com, 12, 108, 120

American Society of Composers, Authors and Publishers (ASCAP), 58

American Stock Exchange (AMEX), 53

Ancor Communications, 89

Andreessen, Marc, 40–41

annual reports, 80, 123

annuities, 140, 141

AOL, 115

Apple Computer, 16, 115

Argentina, 140

Arizona Diamondbacks, 107

Asia, 134, 142, 151

asset(s)
    allocation, 153
    base, 59–60
    capital, 130
    distribution, 145
    financial, 10, 11, 28, 71, 72, 73, 76, 105, 130, 131, 162, 167

    future, 59
    human capital, 2, 4, 103, 108, 162, 166
    intangible, 118, 166, 167
    intellectual, 105
    leveraging, 76
    liquidity, 18, 73, 76, 77
    management, 73, 114, 162, 164
    marketing, 50
    real, 11, 68, 72
    risk, 27, 28, 68
    tangible, 56, 166, 167
    trading, 164–165
    unbundling, 117–118, 166
    valuation, 9, 52
    See also talent

athletes. *See* sports figures and teams

auctions. *See* eBay

authentication issues, 34

autocracy, 129

AutoXchange, 118

baby boomers, 64, 75, 77, 163

Baker Scholars Fund, 50, 55

Bangladesh, 134, 167

Bankers' Trust, 82

bankruptcy, 126, 153, 154, 163
    Chapter 11, 137, 144

bankruptcy (*continued*)
  laws and regulations, 32, 33,
    138, 142–145
banks and banking, 127–128, 153
  commercial, 62
  failures, 138
  investment, 20, 23, 55, 62, 107
  loans, 29
Barnes & Noble, 82
Bay Networks, 115
Beck, Barbara, 104
Bell Atlantic, 121
Bernstein, Peter L., 28
Bessemer, Henry, 40
Best Buy, 115
biotechnology research, 33
Black & Decker, 107
Blair, Tony, 156
Blur (Davis and Meyer), 6
Bombardier snowmobile company,
    88–89
bonds, 26, 48, 51–53, 55, 73, 76, 162,
    163
  corporate, 49
  junk, 26, 47, 72
  personal, 49
  savings, 68
Bowie, David/Bowie Bonds, 46, 47,
    49, 51, 52, 58, 59, 60, 63, 106
brands/branding services, 62, 121,
    122
British Aerospace, 85, 86
Broadcast Music Incorporated
    (BMI), 58–59
brokerage services, 74, 161
Brown, James, 48
budgets/budgeting systems, 84, 97,
    120, 124

Buffet, Warren, 84
Bush, George, 143
business models, 5
business schools, 114

capital
  access to, 46, 133
  allocation, 97, 99
  assets, 130
  cost of, 9, 88, 141
  financial, 9–10, 76, 102, 105,
    129, 133
  gains, 11, 89
  insurance, 85
  intellectual, 29, 38, 62, 105
  investment, 76
  liquidity, 105
  markets, 127, 131, 133, 135, 151,
    152, 154, 166, 167
  real, 76
  retail, 135
  scarcity of, 129
  social, 17, 22–23, 130, 141, 158
  source of, 131
  venture, 52, 97, 99, 120, 143,
    152, 153, 166, 168
  See also tax/tax system: capital
    gains
Capital asset pricing model
    (CAPM), 26
Carnegie, Andrew, 40, 130, 131
Carter, Jimmy, 17
cash flow, 8, 54, 90, 119
Cassell, Justine, 157
Chambers, John, 119
change
  economic, 94, 150, 151

keeping pace with, 94, 99, 100,
        165
    organizational, 94
    technological, 154
Chapter 11. *See* bankruptcy
Charles Schwab & Co., 82
Chase Manhattan Bank, 90
Chile, 135, 140
China, 23, 147, 157
Chrysler Corporation, 144
Cisco Systems, 104, 118, 123
Citigroup, 111, 152, 157
Clark, Jim, 41
class structure, 151
Clinton, Bill, 17, 140
Coca-Cola, 121
Cogen, Jack, 88
Columbia University, 114
commercial paper, 62–63
commissions, trading, 74
communications industry, 6
companies and businesses, 91, 93,
        121, 130, 151
    compensation policies, 107,
        108, 110, 162
    continuous measurement pol-
        icy, 121–124
    corporate cultures, 120, 168
    customers' role in organizational
        design, 98–99
    electronic connections with
        outsiders, 95
    employee investment and, 110,
        111, 113–114, 116
    investment in, 129
    market-based and organized,
        93–94, 95, 96–99, 103, 165
    measurement of intangibles,
        120–121, 166
    measurement of the future,
        119–120
    motivational programs for
        employee wealth, 132–133
    organizational design, 94,
        95–96, 98–99
    pension plans and, 139
    power placement in, 98–99
    return on human capital, 80
    risk management, 80, 82
    risk-taking behavior, 82, 142
    shareholders, 110
    strategic risk units (SRU), 82,
        83, 85, 87–88, 90–91, 165
    training and development prac-
        tices, 102
    virtual, 118
    See also stock options
compensation, 107, 108, 110, 162
competitive advantage, 21
computer industry, 6, 12, 161
Cone, David, 59
connected economy, 2, 5–6, 13, 17,
        23, 93, 129, 166–167
    availability of information and,
        34
    cultural convergence and,
        155–158
    freedom versus order issues, 23,
        33
    future value in, 40
    global, 150, 156
    investment in, 9
    isolation from, 154
    markets of, 17, 18, 31, 42, 110
    production and, 36
    risk and, 17, 36, 73–75, 155

connected economy (*continued*)
  speed in, 5, 6
  See also human capital
connectivity, 2, 7, 42, 96, 156, 157,
    160, 162
  efficiency and, 17–18
  electronic, 123
  of global economy, 153–154
  individual, 22, 151
  Internet, 157
  of technology, 157
Continental Airlines, 144
contracts, 20, 33, 43
copyright, 17, 23
core competencies, 90–91, 97
Corning, 98
corporate raiders, 116–117
cost systems, 22
creativity, 99–100, 106, 151, 155
  investment in, 114, 115
credit, 12, 144, 158
  ratings, 55
  restrictions, 143
credit cards, 54
cryptography/encryption technol-
    ogy, 17, 23
cultural economies, 155–158, 168
currency crises, 8
currency risk, 85
customers, 91, 96, 118, 166
  internal, 97
  investment in, 112, 113
  outsourcing to, 98
  response cycles, 5
cybersex, 16, 17
Cyrix, 96

day trading, 33, 74–75, 169. *See also*
    over-the-counter trading
Death Row Records, 48
debt, 46, 51, 58–59, 63. *See also*
    lending
Dell computers, 118
democracy, 129, 133, 149, 163
Deng Xiaoping, 23
derivatives, 20, 26, 73, 76, 88, 152
de Tocqueville, Alexis, 149, 151
Disney, 82
distributors, 112, 113
Donaldson, Lufkin & Jenrette, 82, 87
Dow Jones Industrial Index, 8, 120,
    153, 154
Dozier, Lamont, 48
Dr. Dre, 48
Drucker, Peter, 95, 131
drug and pharmaceutical industry,
    89–90
DuPont, 87

earning streams
  consistent/predictable, 54, 61
  future, 51, 52, 58, 59, 71, 152
eBay, 18, 19, 30, 49, 52, 76, 120
e-commerce, 5
economic Darwinism, 32, 154
economies of scale, 98
economy/economic systems,
    128–129, 158
  crises, 138
  external, 94
  growth and development, 133,
    135, 154
  planned, 22, 94
  United States, 149–151, 154

See also financial economy/sector; real economy (goods and services)
education, 5, 23, 106, 112
electronic communications networks (ECNs), 152
emigration, 151–152
Employee Retirement Income Security Act (ERISA), 129, 139
employees
    as entrepreneurs, 132
    full-time, 100
    internal, 98
    net worth of, 131–132
    temporary workers, 103, 153
    See also human capital; human resource management; talent
employment, 43, 133
    security, 154, 155, 164
    See also job markets, electronic
encryption standard, 33
Enron Corp., 89
entertainment industry, 51–52, 58
entitlements, 140
entrepreneurship, 33, 114, 130, 133–134, 143, 145, 151, 154
equity, 55, 89, 114, 131
    corporate, 140
    funds, 152
    markets, 141, 167
    ownership of, 128
    pooling of, 15–16
    trading, 53, 74
Ernst & Young, 121
ethical issues, 34
eTrade, 77
e-trading, 18, 19, 74

Europe, 142, 152–153, 154, 155, 156, 168
extranets, 95

Fahnestock, Inc., 47
Federal Reserve, 73, 127, 128
Feldstein, Martin, 140–141
Fidelity Investments, 82
Filo, David, 41
Financial Accounting Standards Board (FASB), 115–116
financial economy/sector, 6–7, 8, 9, 34, 46, 77, 130
    analysts, 12, 77
    instruments, 20, 26, 27, 55, 73, 102
    international, 153–154
    reporting standards, 61
    systems, 152–155
    technology, 64
financial institutions, 33, 90, 103
financial markets, 5, 20, 32, 46, 83, 88, 116, 121–124, 129, 155, 162–163
    corporate tracking stocks and, 87
    efficient, 23
    global, 23
    for human capital, 4, 29–31, 34, 151
    innovation in, 53
financial services industry, 6, 34, 54, 118, 137
Fitzgerald, F. Scott, 72, 73
Ford Motor Company, 96, 118
Forrester Research, 104
Fortune's Global 500, 104
401(k) plans, 7, 13, 67, 70, 77, 112, 130–131, 139, 141, 146, 162, 167

free agency concept, 52, 61–62
freedom, 126, 144, 151, 157
free speech, 23
Frito-Lay North America, 107
futures contracts and markets,
        19–20, 21, 31, 60, 120

Gallie, Joseph, 107–108
gambling, on-line, 33
Gates, Bill, 63, 131
General Electric (GE), 62, 85–86,
        96, 112
General Motors, 83, 117, 118
Generation X, 64, 163
Generation Y, 64–65
Global Positioning System, 15
Goldman, Sachs, 45, 62
goods and services. *See* real economy
        (goods and services)
Grameen Bank, 134
Great Depression, 138
greenmail, 117
Greenspan, Alan, 8–9

Harvard Business School, 142
health care, 29, 141–142, 155, 163
        insurance, 64, 67, 69–70, 75,
                129, 138, 139–141
        tax, 146–148
Healtheon, 41
hedges, 20, 27, 60, 112, 137, 150, 165
Hewlett-Packard, 94, 100
Hill, Grant, 59
HMOs, 69
Hobbs, Thomas, 22
Holland, Brian, 48

Holland, Edward, 48
Hollywood Stock Exchange (HSX),
        51–52, 55, 59, 77
Howard University, 55
human capital, 5, 6, 9, 21–22, 23,
        40, 43, 51–53, 56, 99–100,
        168
        as asset, 2, 4, 103, 108
        –backed securities, 102–105
        development, 106, 112
        financial market for, 4, 29–31,
                34, 151
        investment in, 43–44, 47, 50–51,
                61, 110, 111, 116, 118, 166
        as liability, 108
        markets, 2, 53, 56, 60, 111, 112,
                115, 130, 151, 158, 162–163
        measurement of, 30
        microlending and, 133–135
        migration of, 41–42
        monetizing of, 116–118
        as opportunity, 51–53
        packaging, 118, 163, 166
        pooling/bundling of, 53, 60–61
        return on, 27, 56
        risk, 38, 139
        trading, 63, 75, 103, 108, 118, 163
        unbundling of, 117–118, 166
        valuation of, 40–41, 56, 60
        See also connected economy;
                employees; intellectual
                capital; securitization: of
                human capital; stock
                options; talent
human resource management, 166
        employee quality and, 105–108
        human capital–backed securi-
                ties, 102–105

output measurement/perform-
   ance reviews, 106–107
risk versus talent, 105
securitization of human capital,
   108
See also intellectual capital

IBM, 106
IDEO, 97
income, 131, 166
   distribution, 153
   earned, 10, 11, 13
   family, 130
   versus net worth, 10, 162
   securitization, 163
   unearned, 10–11, 13
   versus wealth, 145–146
   See also tax/tax system: income;
      wealth
increasing returns concept, 9
India, 21–22
Individual Financial Accounting
      Standards Board (IFASB),
      61
Indonesia, 8
industrial technologies, 98, 128
INET conferences, 133
inflation, 9, 70, 72
information, 2, 5, 34, 64, 95, 118
   access, 23, 34, 98, 122
   competitive, 31
   costs, 74
   economy, 9, 162
   financial, 12
   flow, 157
   market, 18
   services, 6

standardization of, 108
technologies, 98, 129
initial public offerings, 152
innovation, 100, 135, 143, 152, 156
insurance, 15, 16, 26, 29, 73, 76, 127,
   162
   corporate, 81, 82, 84, 85–87
   health care, 64, 67, 70, 75, 129,
      138, 141–142, 146–148
   life, 138
   retirement, 163
   risk and, 28, 67–68, 71, 72,
      85–87, 138, 139
   social, 126, 138–139, 142, 148
   unemployment, 139, 155
   workers' compensation, 54, 138
intellectual capital, 6, 41, 62, 63, 65,
   102, 105, 110, 112, 114, 118,
   131, 163
   access to, 133
   monetization of, 113
   ownership of, 130
   trading, 103, 116, 166
   See also human capital; human
      resource management
intellectual property, 40, 54, 114
interest rates, 8, 48, 143
intermediaries, 18, 62, 74, 75, 82,
   103
internal transfer prices, 94, 97
International Labor Organization
      (ILO), 133, 134
Internet, 4, 5, 95–96, 133, 150, 162
   access, 156–157
   companies and businesses, 84
   diversity of opinion on, 157–158
   elimination of intermediaries
      and, 74

Internet (*continued*)
  market efficiency of, 19
  start-ups, 73, 120
  stock trading, 18
  transactions, 34, 59
  Web directory, 41
  See also job markets, electronic
intranets, 95
Intuit, 102
investment(s), 7, 11, 29, 32, 62, 68,
    76, 131, 146, 168
  accounts, government-assisted,
    135, 140–141
  accounts, private, 140
  collateralized, 154
  diversification, 47
  fluidity, 73–74
  on future earning streams, 59
  in human capital, 43–44, 47,
    50–51, 61, 62, 110, 111, 116,
    118, 166
  in Internet companies, 84
  long-term, 61
  portfolios, 7, 71–73, 75, 76, 77
  real estate, 71–72, 73, 130
  risk, 17, 26, 27, 28, 46, 52, 53,
    71–72, 91
  in tracking stocks, 87
  unregulated high-risk, 33
IPOs, 4, 26, 41, 50, 62, 77
IRAs, 13, 67, 70, 141, 162, 167
ISP (Internet Service Provider), 30
Israel, 151

Jackson, Phil, 105
Japan, 152, 153, 154, 156, 168
Jefferson, Thomas, 22

job markets, electronic, 30–31,
    42–43, 99, 104–105, 163
Jobs, Steve, 16
Johnson, Randy, 107
Jordan, Michael, 39, 53, 63
Junior Summit, 157
junk bonds, 26, 47, 72
"just-in-time" production, 96
J&W Seligman, 32

Kao, John, 100
Karlin, Bob, 102
keiretsu, 113
Kennedy, John F., 93
Keogh plans, 13, 70, 130
Kidzbank, 157
King, Stephen, 41
Kinko's, 96, 97
Kinsella, John, 30
Kleiner Perkins Caufield & Byers,
    45–46
knowledge economy, 132
knowledge workers. *See* human
    capital; human resource
    management; intellectual
    capital; talent
Krasilovsky, William, 54–55

labor costs, 122
LaFeber, Maarten, 52
laws and regulations, 148, 161
    bankruptcy, 32, 33, 138, 142–145
    concerning wealth, 126, 130, 138
    contract, 33
    property, 143
    workers' compensation, 54, 138

Lazio soccer club (Italy), 48
LBOs, 26
Leaf, Ryan, 59
lending, 46, 143, 145, 153, 154
    financial, 134
    microlending, 133–135, 141, 167
    subsidized, 130
Lenin, 22, 128
liability
    human capital, 108
    limited, 142–143
    See also risk listings
liquidity, 8
    of assets, 18, 73, 76, 77
    of capital, 105
    of markets, 18, 49
    of wealth, 11
loans. *See* lending
local area networks, 123
Locke, John, 22
Long Term Capital Management
        hedge fund, 144, 150
Lorenzo, Frank, 144
Los Angeles Lakers, 59
Lotus, 106

Machinists Union, 144
Maddux, Greg, 59
Maffei, Greg, 116
Malaysia, 8, 85, 86, 154
management, 5, 84, 91, 165. *See
        also* human resource
        management
Manning, Payton, 41
Manpower, Inc., 103
market economies, 94, 130
market(s), 2, 18, 22, 106, 164

access to, 19
capital, 20, 29–30, 77, 84, 97,
        127, 131, 133, 135, 146, 151,
        152, 154, 166, 167, 168
competition, 96
of connected economy, 42
connectivity of, 12
continuous price adjustment
        and, 18–19
democratization of, 75, 130
efficient, 2, 17–20, 23, 31, 53, 81,
        95, 99, 100, 103, 110, 111,
        114, 121, 130, 154–155, 157,
        158, 168
electronic, 30–31, 42, 74, 76,
        103, 118
entry price, 9–10
equity, 141
external, 97
feedback, 107, 121, 123
flexibility, 150, 154, 168
future, 19–20, 21, 31, 60, 120
global risk, 30, 31
intellectual capital, 63
international capital, 146
labor, 4–5, 30–31, 42–43, 104,
        110, 168
liquidity, 18, 49
open/free, 19, 22
research, 121
risk, 17, 26, 32, 43, 48, 158
secondary, 18, 61
testing/simulation models, 84, 121
transparent, 18
value, 22, 41–42
See also financial markets;
        human capital: markets;
        job markets, electronic

Marketsite, 118

Marx, Karl, 126, 128, 167

Massachusetts Institute of Technology (MIT), 157

McKinsey, 112

means tests, 148

measurement and control systems, 119–124

media properties, 51–52

Medicaid, 139, 142

medical ethics, 19

medical savings accounts (MSAs), 141–142, 148

Medicare, 142, 147, 148

Meeker, Mary, 30

Mercata, 19

meritocracy, 129, 167

Merrill Lynch, 48, 77

Mexico, 8, 140

Michigan University, 114

MicroAge, 121

microlending, 133–135, 141, 167

Microsoft, 9, 53, 87, 116
    stock option plans, 131–132

middle class. *See* wealth: middle-class

Middle East, 157

Milken, Michael, 50

money market accounts, 74

Monster.com, 30, 42, 60, 77, 99, 103, 104

Moody's Investor Service, 47, 48, 49

moral hazard concept, 32–33, 143

Morgan Stanley, 30

mortgages, 46, 50, 51, 54, 55, 76

Motown record label, 48, 55

movie industry, 51–52, 123

Mulgan, Geoff, 156

music industry, 58–59

mutual funds, 11, 28, 29, 55, 60, 61, 63, 72–77, 118, 127–128, 131, 139, 145

Myers, Mike, 52

Myint, Hla, 133

nanotechnology, 16, 17

National Association and Securities Dealers Association Quotations (NASDAQ), 53, 60, 74, 152

NatSource, 88

Netscape Communications, 40–41, 115

networked communities, 42

net worth, 11
    of employees, 131–132
    versus income, 10, 162

New York Stock Exchange (NYSE), 18, 53

New York University, 114

NFO Worldwide, 75

Nikkei Index, 153, 154

Nokia cell phone company, 156

Nomura Securities, 48

Northwestern University, 114

options, 72, 89
    real, 90, 91
    See also stock options

Oracle, 115, 118

order concept, 23, 33, 126, 144, 151

Organization for Economic Cooperation and Development (OECD), 146

outsourcing, 41, 96, 97, 98, 165
over-the-counter trading, 53, 88.
    See also day trading
ownership, 128–130, 131, 132–133,
    143, 153
Oxford Health Plans, 115
Ozzie, Ray, 106

Pasteur, Louis, 12
patents, 40, 113–114, 166
pension plans/funds, 12, 13, 28, 29,
    70, 75, 76, 127, 130, 131, 139,
    140, 146, 155, 163, 164
    funded, 139
    private, 140
PepsiCo, 107
performance
    future, 110
    measurement and manage-
      ment, 120, 124
    reviews, 106–107, 124
Personal Data Bank (PDB)
    accounts, 124
personal retirement account (PRA),
    141
personal securities. *See* securitiza-
    tion: of human capital
Peru, 140
Peters, Tom, 50
Picasso principle, 21, 28
Pilgrim Baxter, 32
piracy, 34
plutocracy, 128, 129
point solution programs, 137
political freedom, 22
Pollan, Stephen, 64
pooling

    of equity, 15–16
    of risk, 16, 46, 50, 59, 68, 82,
      134
    of talent, 31, 49, 50–51, 58,
      60–61
pornography, child, 23
Postman, Andrew, 46
poverty line, 134
price
    entry, 9–10
    market adjustment, 18–19
    speculation, 138
    spot, 122
    strike, 115–116
privacy issues, 17, 23
private equity funds, 32
probability theory, 28
process industries, 123
production/products, 5, 6, 36, 122,
    129
    control of, 128
    cycle, 106
    ownership of means of, 130, 143
productivity, 122, 138, 148
profits, 128, 145, 169
    future streams, 110, 114
property rights/private property, 23,
    129, 130, 142, 143
public policy, 138
    laws and regulations, 142–145
    social insurance, 126, 138–139,
      142, 148
    social security, 64, 70, 75, 129,
      138, 139–141, 146, 163
    See also tax/tax system
Pullman, David, 55
Pullman Group, 47, 48, 53, 54, 55
Putnam Investments, 32

Radio Free Europe, 157
Reagan, Ronald, 143
real economy (goods and services),
    6, 8, 9, 23, 34
    futures markets and, 19–20
real estate, 7–8, 43, 71–72, 73, 102, 130
Real Madrid football club, 48
Reliance Insurance Company, 82,
    86–87, 138
repricing programs, 115–116
research and development, 113
resource allocation, 29, 99
restructuring, 41
retainers, 115
retirement plans. *See* pension
    plans/funds
revenue streams, 46, 47–48, 50. *See
    also* earning streams
reward systems, 110. *See also*
    compensation
risk, 96, 98, 151, 157, 158
    corporate. *See* risk, corporate
    external, 143
    financial, 91, 142, 145
    future wealth and, 120
    individual. *See* risk, individual
    interchangeable, 103
    isolation of, 152
    management, 43, 144
    as opportunity, 148, 151, 162
    protection, 151
    real, 142, 145
    societal/global, 141, 150
    -taking behavior, 82, 142,
        145–146, 154
    trading, 64, 110, 160
risk, corporate, 10, 13, 27, 51, 82, 85,
    88–89, 96, 153, 166–167

analysis, 82, 83, 111, 113–114
goal setting and, 84–85
government-managed, 144
insurance for, 81, 82, 84
isolation of, 82–83, 85, 87, 114
management, 82, 84, 88, 90–91,
    122, 165
as opportunity, 83–85, 87–88, 165
outsourcing of, 91
packaging of, 85–86, 87
pooling/bundling of, 82, 86–87
return on human capital and,
    27, 111
shareholders and, 83, 84, 86
speculative, 137
strategic risk units (SRU), 82,
    83, 85, 87–88, 90–91, 165
trading, 88–90
risk, individual, 25–26, 38, 60, 138,
    139, 153, 156
analysis, 2, 10, 16, 27–28, 51, 55,
    69–70, 74–75, 77, 83,
    151–152, 162
aversion, 68–69, 71, 76, 134–135,
    138, 143
comfort with, 71, 72–73,
    75–78
connected economy and, 17, 33,
    73–75
diversification, 16, 26, 47, 48,
    51, 134
financial, 11, 28–29, 52, 68, 70,
    139, 163
government-managed, 139
health, 146–148
integrated, 137, 139
investment, 46, 52, 53
lending, 46, 126

management, 16, 43, 67, 70–73,
    76–78, 137, 164
markets and, 17, 20, 26, 30, 32,
    43, 48
moral hazard, 32–33, 143
as opportunity, 2, 26–29, 32–36,
    34, 36, 69, 72, 73, 75
packaging of, 164
pooling/bundling of, 16, 46, 50,
    59, 68, 134
portfolios, 71–73, 77
protection (safety nets), 2,
    27–28, 36, 126, 139, 162, 163
securitization of, 20, 36
-taking behavior, 152, 163
trading, 7–8, 20, 26–27, 33, 34,
    47, 64, 70, 72, 164
transfer of, 48–49
of wealth creation, 138
See also human resource man-
    agement
Risk Rationalization Accounts, 78
Road Ahead, The (Gates), 131
Rodman, Dennis, 59
Roosevelt, Teddy, 22
royalties, 40, 47, 48, 54, 58–59
Rubin, Robert, 26
Russia, 22, 32, 150, 152

Sablowsky, Robert, 47
Sahlman, Bill, 142–143
salespeople, 107
satellites, 158
savings, 11, 68, 71, 130, 140, 146, 168
savings and loan industry, 143–144
savings bonds, 68
scholarships, 148

schools, public, 123–124
screening mechanisms for insurance
    coverage, 147
Sears, 122
securities/securities industry, 75,
    94, 163
    financial, 16, 17, 19
securitization, 20, 38, 46–50, 55, 60,
    76–77, 102–105, 108, 118, 164
    asset base for, 59–60
    of debt, 58–59, 63
    generational shifts, 63–65
    of human capital, 49–50, 53–54,
        60, 63, 76–77, 108, 164
    of ideas, 113–114, 116
    of income, 163
    institutionalization of the
        exchange, 60–63
    of property rights, 54–55
    of risk, 20, 36
    of talent, 55, 110–111
security issues, 23
Sega, 157
self-employment, 43, 61–62, 96
Service, Paul, 54–55
service industry, 5, 6, 51
Shakur, Tupac, 48
shareholders, 84, 86, 110, 115, 116
Sharpe, William, 26
Silent Generation, 63–64
Silicon Graphics, 41
Silicon Valley, 42, 45, 62, 130, 153,
    156
Singapore, 21, 156, 158
Snoop Doggy Dogg, 48
social security, 64, 70, 75, 129, 138,
    139–141, 163
    tax, 146

Social Security Act, 138

society/social systems, 5, 13, 32, 155

software/software industry, 5, 6, 9, 22, 23, 33, 106, 116, 123, 161

Soros, 152

Sosa, Sammy, 39

special-purpose vehicle (SPV), 54

speed, 2, 5, 6, 99

sponsorship, 48

sports figures and teams, 39, 48, 52–53, 58, 59, 60, 107

spot pricing, 122

Standard & Poor, 49

standards and practices, 60, 61, 77, 108, 154, 155

Starck, Phillippe, 41

start-ups, 15, 19, 52, 62, 97

  funding of, 112, 114

  Internet, 73, 120

Stephenson, Neal, 40

stock markets/exchanges, 51–52, 53, 71, 73, 84, 145

  international, 152–154

stock options, 27, 51–53, 70, 109–113, 115–116, 130, 131–132

  cost of, 112

  shareholders and, 110, 115

  strike price for, 115–116

stock(s), 26, 51, 71–73, 75, 76, 127, 162, 163

  day trading, 33, 74–75, 169

  high-risk, 74

  Internet companies and, 84

  over-the-counter trading, 53, 88

  prices, 8–9, 10, 88, 122

  purchase programs, 132

  tracking, 87

trading, 18, 108

stop-loss orders, 122

strategic business unit (SBU), 82, 83, 98

strategic risk units (SRU), 82, 83, 85, 87–88, 90–91, 165

subsidiaries, 87

Sumitomo, 152

Sun Microsystems, 89, 90

suppliers, 112, 113, 118, 165

surplus, 128, 129, 135, 141

Swatch, 157

Sweden, 153, 155, 158

syndication, 52

talent, 82, 102, 129, 130, 163, 167

  as asset, 9, 38

  -backed securities, 55

  bidding for, 21, 104, 107–108, 116

  leveraging of, 39–40, 43

  mobility of, 42–43, 100, 112, 115

  political atmosphere for, 129

  pooling/bundling of, 31, 49, 50–51, 58, 60–61

  securitization of, 55, 110–111

  See also human capital; human resource management

Talent Market, 30–31

tariffs, protective, 155

tax/tax system, 5, 13, 126, 129, 130, 145–148, 163, 168

  breaks, 139

  capital gains, 129, 138, 145–146

  codes, 137–138, 148

  consumption, 138, 146, 168

  corporate, 146

deductions, 146
double, 146
income, 129, 140, 145–147, 168
laws and regulations, 141–142
payroll, 146
progressive, 129, 146–147
sales, 33
social security, 139–140, 141, 146
value-added, 146
on wealth, 145
wellness, 146–148
Taylor, Jeff, 99, 104
telephone services, 161
Texas Instruments, 83
Thailand, 8
Thatcher, Margaret, 22
The Medicines Company (TMC),
89–90
Thermoelectron, 98
Thomas H. Lee Co., 32
Tihany, Adam, 41
time sharing, 20
Times Mirror Co., 86, 87, 90
Torré, Joe, 105
Toyota, 98
transaction costs, 74
transfers, 34, 88
Treasury bills, 27, 162
Trevino, Lee, 52
Trudeau, Gary, 57
Trump, Donald, 144
Turkey, 151

unbundling of human capital,
117–118, 166
underemployment, 134
underwriting, 110

unemployment, 138, 155
unions, 12, 42, 54, 129, 138, 144
United Kingdom, 22, 155, 156
University of California, Los
Angeles, 114
Unleashing the Killer App (Downes
and Mui), 98
U.S. Steel, 9, 40

value, 5
creation, 9, 143, 152, 165
flexibility of, 122
future, 40
of individuals, 41–42
migration, 41, 118
risk and, 143
voting, 129

Wales, 22
Waller, Fats, 55
Wal-Mart, 123
warrants, 89
watermark system, electronic, 34
wealth, 2, 4, 5, 6–13, 14, 22, 160
accumulation, 4, 7–10, 12, 13,
14, 28, 64, 72, 73, 128, 138,
154, 168
control of, 4, 12–13, 14, 132, 154
creation, 4, 5, 7–10, 11, 13, 17,
31, 32, 72, 129, 134, 141, 169
democratization of, 127
distribution/flow, 4, 7, 10–12, 14,
112, 131, 154, 157
financial, 7, 14, 73, 130
future, 13, 43, 126
gap, owners/workers, 128–129

wealth, (*continued*)

generation of, 130–131

investment of, 138, 146

management, 12–13, 123

middle-class, 11, 13, 28, 34, 73,
77, 126, 130, 131, 167–168

migration of, 11, 132, 164

protection, 64, 72, 76

real, 7, 8, 14

redistribution, 145

relative, 133

tax, 145

trading of, 43

virtual exchange of, on the
Internet, 59

versus income, 145–146

See also income

Weill, Sanford, 111

Woods, Tiger, 53

World Bank, 134

Yahoo!, 41, 120

Yale University, 114

Yang, Jerry, 41

Yew, Lee Kwan, 156

Ziff-Davis, 87

About the Authors

STAN DAVIS is an independent author and public speaker based in Boston as well as a Senior Research Fellow at the Ernst & Young Center for Business Innovation in Cambridge, Massachusetts. He is well known as a visionary business thinker who advises leading companies and fast-growing enterprises around the world. This is his tenth book. Some of his earlier influential books include *Blur, Future Perfect,* 2020 *Vision,* and *The Monster Under the Bed.*

CHRISTOPHER MEYER is a partner of Ernst & Young and the Director of the Ernst & Young Center for Business Innovation, which researches the emerging issues facing business. He is also President of Bios GP, Inc., Ernst & Young's venture in the application of complexity theory to business. With more than twenty years of experience in general management and economic consulting, he is an authority on the evolution of the information economy and its impact on business. He is a regular columnist in *Business* 2.0 and the coauthor of *Blur.*